Janice
Thank you for
supporting me

A Myriad of Emotions

Michelle Larks

Michelle Larks

EbonyEnergy Publishing
Chicago, Illinois

EbonyEnergy Publishing
Permissions Department
P.O. Box 43476
Chicago, IL 60643-0476

ISBN: 0-9722795-2-0
Library of Congress Control Number: 2003102501

Cover Art: Darril Fountain
Cover Design: Na'Tasha D. Smith
Editor: Robert N. Stephenson
Technical Support: Rasaki Solebo

To every woman who has been involved in an "illicit relationship" or even contemplated going there.

To every family member and friend who has supported someone in need.

To every woman who has the courage to love when the deck is stacked against her. It is better to try than not to try!

A Special Dedication
To All The Sistahs
Who Have Been There
And Done That!

Dedication

**This Book Is Dedicated
To My
Daughters**

**I Love
Both Of You
Very Much**

Mom

Acknowledgments

Many thanks to my 'Father Above' for guiding me and allowing me the opportunity to tell my story. Hopefully there are others waiting to be told.

Thanks to all my Moms; Mary Brown, Jean Harris and Bertha Larks. You've all provided me with wisdom and life lessons to be shared.

Thanks to all my siblings, Big Sis loves you! A special thanks to my *sister girlfriends*. You willingly shared your thoughts and advice during this endeavor.

Thanks to Cheryl Katherine Wash for encouragement and becoming a mentor of sorts. Most of all thanks for helping me attain a dream come true. Thanks Darril Fountain for your beautiful artwork and stepping in when I needed you the most. Thanks Robert N. Stephenson, my editor for giving me courage to pursue the dream.

Most of all I owe many thanks to my husband Fredrick, For being patient, completing my share of the chores and not complaining at the lack of quality time as I worked fast and furious on this book!
Michelle

Table of Contents

Foreword

This could be about any woman, young or old. It could be a story about you. Many women have traveled this road I have. There is no doubt that many more will follow in my steps. A Myriad of Emotions is a story that transcends race. This is my story.

I was your quiescent 'Super Woman', wearing many hats that so many of us modern women try to wear. You know what I mean, wife, mother, lover, employee, sister and friend.

My life was stuck in neutral. My hats became heavy upon my head. After attaining many goals I had set for myself soon I found myself in a loveless marriage. It ended in divorce.

Over the next two years I began an affair with a man who wasn't married from a legal standpoint that is. But was involved in a committed relationship. He told me the usual lines that men often do, when they know they are doing something wrong or looking for excuses. She didn't understand him. They were two people sharing the bills and sometimes the same bed.

My life has been complex and simple, cold and emotion filled. I have lived the gambit of experiences and ordeals. Through it all, I wrote poetry and kept journals of those days I lived being who I am.

One day while rummaging through an old bag, I discovered pages and pages of my writings. I was taken aback by how much I had written about my relationship. So moved by my discovery that I decided to share these experiences with you *My Sistahs*.

Ahh...Sweet Beginnings

_In The Beginning.....

Some say the best part of a relationship, when each is
on his/her best behavior. As we slowly
or quickly discover each other's nuances.
It's all good at the start that sweet, magical time.
Each trying so very hard to please each other.
Or when he's trying to reel you in!

What You Mean To Me

The sun and the moon rolled into one
You've stolen my heart that's what you've done
You've made this world a better place
I see love in your eyes on your sweet face

You are my first thought when I awake
This love is true on my life I'd stake
I say a little prayer for you at night
I love you with all my being strength and might

Just say the word and I'll come to you
This love is everlasting glorious and true
I'll be there for you a promise I'll keep
Feelings run so long and so very deep

Words can't adequately describe what I feel for you
Everyday is an adventure wonderful and new
Just knowing there is someone who is there for me
I'm not alone there is a 'we'

I don't know why God has blessed me so
All I can say is I'll take it and more
You see my love you mean the world to me
I love you so much can't you see

Your Smile

Your smile warms a place in my heart
It says to me girl we'll never part
It makes me feel joy when I'm feeling down
How happy I am with this love I found

Your smile says don't worry I'll make it better
Regardless of day night clear or stormy weather
It's the one thing in life I can depend on
When life's trials and tribulations get me down

Your smile says baby you're the best
You're head and shoulders above the rest
It holds promises of good things to come
Excitement joy pleasure and fun

Your smile says woman I'm Here For You
To support you in everything little thing you do
A steady presence in my life
Helping me overcome adversities sorrows and strife

Yes your smile it surely makes my day
Sending waves of love along my way
Keep on doing what you're doing to me
Smiling at me making me feel loved you see

I'm Here For You

When the going gets rough I'll be there for you
Helping support you in every little thing you do
In good times and even bad yes I'm here
Cause that's what love is all about my dear

When the job kids and just life get you down
All you have to do is call and I promise I'll be around
Just sit yourself gently down in the chair
I'll massage your body run my fingers through your hair

I'll smooth those frowns and wrinkles from your face
Let me take you my love to a better place
Rest your head upon my shoulder
That's what lovers are for

Material things I can't always give to you
But you can believe my best I will do
There are not many things in life that prove to be true
One thing you can depend on is Baby I'm here for you

A Love So Strong

My man gives me strength to make it through the day
Sending waves of optimism along my way
I try not to let circumstances get me down
Cause in just a little while his love I'll be around

We have our ups and downs good times and bad
We get on each other nerves and make each other mad
But when I think of that precious smiling face
My heart beats at a very rapid pace

With a love so strong you can work out anything
This man he sends me makes my heart sing
That special love a tender loving touch
I get weak cause I want that man so much

Love makes me feel there is nothing I can't do
The strong ties that bind together *me and you*
A love so strong is what keeps me going
Him beside me confident wise and knowing

Commitment

After a passage of time I'm ready to take the next step
Towards a true and lasting love my heart felt
I knew from the start we were meant to be together
Through the sunshine rain and stormy weather

Bit by bit you crept into my heart
We were meant to be forever never apart
You see I'd given up on love so long ago
Loneliness had become my enemy, my foe

I'd pray to just make it through the day
I was totally convinced love would never come my way
Then there you stepped right into my life
You calmed my fears soothed me and made it alright

I thank God for sending you to me
He saw a heart in need of love you see
He knew what I wanted best
He took care of it all the rest

Yes I'm ready to step it up a notch or two
You just being you and the things you do
I am yours for as long as you want
It's the little things you do that count

Sexual Interludes

Of Course the Sex was off the hook!

You know I have to admit that I was so scared the first time we did the do. Let's be honest I wasn't a firm twenty-something. Didn't even come close to any man's wet dream. Would he enjoy it? What if he didn't? Could I even make it over the mountain and attain the almighty orgasm? Hell, I didn't have anything resembling sexy lingerie in my closet or dresser drawer. I was in a dilemma, what's a Sistah to do? Well, I took a trip to the mall to visit Ms. Vickie. She had just what I needed for that special occasion, 'the love fest.' The thought of taking of my clothes off in front of my lover simply petrified me. I hadn't experienced the physical part of loving in such a long time. There was no need to worry nor was there cause to fret. My lover awakened all those feelings and brought me back to life. He reeled me in, made his moves. My toes curled, he had me swooning, yelling and screaming. Then I was gone......

What You Do To Me

You have released so many feeling in me
It's all pretty scary and new don't you see
I said I'd never let another man get close
Taking me from me all that I value the most

You came along and did what no other had done before
Healed a heart that was broken bruised and sore
Tore down my defenses smashed the walls
You only have to beckon ask or call

Slowly but surely you've brought me back to life
Making me forget worries troubles and strife
Passion jealously emotions you have aroused
Keep it coming the flames you'd better not douse

I didn't think my heart would ever sing again
You captured me with the joy you bring
I don't know how long all this will last
You my love are truly the best

I'm doing and feeling things I never thought I would
I never imagined it or even knew I could
What you do to me is truly a sight to behold
I hope the feeling keeps growing and never gets old

This Thing Love

Love has turned my life upside down
I'm walking on air my feet never touch the ground
You're on my mind before I go to sleep at night
First thing in the morning and it feels so right

I see your face in the corners of my mind
You are truly unique to me one of a kind
When I think of you my knees get weak and shake
This thing love it's for real no fake

I find myself singing smiling and humming
When I know you're on your way to me just coming
That private special loving look you give to me
Love made us one I'm ready let us be

I want to shout proclaim to the world he's mine
You're a jewel to me tender and kind
Thanks for letting me share your life
This thing called love it feels so right

The Heat Between Me and You

A liquid fire burns between the two of us
That thin line between love and lust
Starting with a simple kiss from you
Traveling through my body I don't know what to do

It doesn't take much a look can ignite it
The fire is raging the match has been lit
A simple loving touch a tender caress
I want to tear off my clothes and get undressed

That smothering look of desire burning in your eyes
Waves of desire travel down to my thighs
I get damp and oh so wet
To that special part of your body I want to get

Your hands touching and feeling along my body
I want to dance with you at the lover's party
Feeling the heat from my head down to my toes
I want you and long to scream *more... more...more...*

Tasting you upon my mouth touching you with my hands
Pushing pulsating I feel it coming yes I can
Something so soft can become oh so hard
Entering me filling me leaving me breathless and hot

In and out of my center the core of me
The secret true essence of me you feel and see
Yes there's a flame raging between me and you
I want you so bad I just don't know what to do

Stroking the Fire

I'm so very hot and I want it so bad
Don't make me wait and don't make me mad
Our clothes they just seem to be in the way
Let's tear them off is that alright is it okay

Yes make me feel good and I'll do the same for you
You know how to do so well that thing that you do
Kiss my lips until they're swollen sore and raw
Feelings like this should be banned plain outlawed

The foreplay just drives me wild
Put those buttons just hit the dial
There's a liquid fire burning inside
I'm so wet and this desire I can't hide

Come on now yeah put it right there
Bring the bear back home to its lair
Just a little while longer and I'll come
I'm not shy or scared no I won't run

Oh that simply feels marvelous
We fit perfectly together the two of us
Told you if you do me I'll do you
It's off the hook, the heat between me and you

Touch Me There

Just touch me yeah feel me there
Build those sensations mess up my hair
Stroke me yes caress it do it right
Let's rock it baby all through the night

Play my body like the Stradivarius it is
Work those lips shower my body with kisses
You know how to do it come on put it right there
Show me you want it and I'll show you how much I care

Your fingers ooh just let them roam
Come on lover bring it on home
Your touch simply drives me wild
Keep on make me crazy open it up make it smile

Don't stop now I can feel it building down from the core
I just want it all give it to me more, more, more
Oh I'm coming and it feels so good
You touch me as only you could

Descend Into A Myriad of Emotions

As you can tell I had stars in my eyes...

Brother was doing a job on me I can't lie. He had me... I was gone. It's been said all good things come to an end and my time was almost up.

Promises were made that couldn't be kept. It was time for him to step up to the plate. Some of us we've been there. We know how the story goes.

I was the other woman, at the beginning of this relationship. I warned him over and over again. That I wouldn't, couldn't, stay in a triangle. Not for very long anyway. I was home alone it seemed most of the time. We couldn't spend any time together, especially the holidays. I had my set time. Yes my allocated hours, Monday through Friday...nine to five working hours. After all that time in my marriage I just couldn't accept that slot any more. He kept saying he was working on his situation. Years went by and you can guess the rest. You know how these things work out in the end

The Real Me

Why do you close your eyes to the real me inside
Why must my love and emotions I hide
What have I done for you to hurt me so much
My only sin is in being weak for your touch

Must you turn away from me after my love you'd won
I thought you were the man and my searching was done
Life has a funny way of playing tricks
Now my poor broken heart it needs to be fixed

I really didn't want it to be this way
I thought we gotten through the night to the day
Can't you see it hurts me so damn bad
I feel so desolate and I'm so damn sad

Sometimes I pray Lord give me one good day
And only good things pass my way
The real me locked up in here I want to come out
I want my spirits uplifted moving and about

Open your eyes take a good look at the real me
Quiet my heart and just let me be
Free me from this awful pain
So my sorrow can flee like the wind-blown rain

Trusting You

Trust is such a small five-letter word
Sometimes vague and subtle like a soaring bird
Trust should be so easy yet I find it's so hard
It's elusive to me like finding a lucky card

I am not a suspicious person by nature
We all start with a clean slate it's what comes later
You know like when you said you'd call me tonight
I sat by the phone wouldn't let it out of sight

The times you said Baby, I'm on my way to see you
So far you have yet that to do
I asked if we could go places together sometimes
You said yes but I'm still waiting for that first time

My trust began eroding withering then started dying
You couldn't be honest you were untruthful just plain lying
Just once I'd like to hear you say
It's your turn baby we'll do it your way

I know quite well it's not coming true
It feels me with sadness makes me so blue
It took a long time for reality to sink into my brain
Trust began fleeing like water seeping down the drain

The War In My Head

There's a war going on in my head
I wonder what kind of trip I'm being led
I have good days and bad
At times I'm okay then I feel sad

I have to play guessing games all of the time
I never know if I'm winning or losing half the time
I'm so tired I just want my tender heart to mend
I want the war in my head to end

Does he or doesn't he will he or won't he
Put me out of this misery just let me be
Is there a place for me in your heart
If not end the sorrow just let us part

One voice the negative one says fool no he don't
One day he will then the next one he won't
The positive voice says you know he cares
And I know in my heart we were meant to be a happy pair

Back and forth voices going round my head all the time
Talking singing rapping and rhyming
Some days the positive one loses the negative one wins
I get a headache I want the war in my head to end

Just Talk to Me

Why can't you just tell me what I need to know
Are you with me or will you just go
I don't like these feelings the uncertainty
Free me let me go just let me be

I had high hopes from the very start
When it became apparent you had stolen my heart
But I now I ache I feel so damn blue
Cause you won't talk to me and tell me what's true

I've suspected for a long time that things weren't right
I tried so hard to fight the feelings with all my might
But now I'm tired and I feel so weak
Just talk to me it's the truth I now seek

I won't go crazy and act like a clown
I hate this always feeling so down
If you want out that's all you have to say
So I can continue the rest of my days

Just talk to me I promise I won't bite
I promise to let you go without a whimper or a fight
Your happiness is important to me too
I want to do what's best in the long run for me and you

I Should Have Known Better

I didn't listen when my head said to leave you alone
I thought I could handle it, be mature and fully-grown
I couldn't imagine a time when we wouldn't be together
Not one entire day nor one night not now or ever

There's a tiny piece of time of the day allocated to me
Not one hour earlier or later is all I get don't you see
I have an assigned role to play in this relationship
Don't complain and don't ever give you any lip

I should have know better than to even try
Relationships can't be based on lies
My heart knew better and kept saying 'you can't do this'
But for your love I yearned it's you I missed

I thought not doing things together wouldn't bother me
I lied to myself closed my eyes and didn't want to see
The simple things most couples take for granted
A phone call drinks going out to dinner and dancing

I should've known you couldn't really be mine
So for a true love I search and if I'm lucky I'll find
The man out there who can solely be for there for me
You see if he cheats on her he'll definitely cheat on me

The Going Gets Tough

Well Sistahs, the end was in sight...

as the Temptations sang, 'right around the corner, just across the tracks'. I knew it and could feel it. Sadly, I just didn't want to believe it. I was in a place that was filled with pain and I hurt so damn much. I asked myself how something so good could go bad in just two short years. I kept trying to get into his head and find out what he was thinking. I needed to know what he wanted and where he wanted to go with the relationship. It seemed the harder I pushed the more he backed off. He offered excuse after excuse. Sadly and ironically I just wasn't hearing him. I asked him over and over again if he was tired of me. Did he find the relationship too stifling? It got to the point each day become heavy laden. I felt like I was walking through an ocean wearing lead boots. I tried to find my way ashore. The time was one of the darkest periods in my life. When he opened up, he still insisted, the relationship was fine. He just needed time and time became a precious commodity. I just couldn't go on.......

Got Me Some Blues

I got the blues so damn bad it hurts
I can't seem to make it right though I work and work
Still nothing remains except heartache and pain
Tears flow down my face burning like acid rain

The blues got me locked up in balls and chains
There will be no winning no happiness no gain
That man he just don't want to be mine
Peace of mind it eludes me I can't seem to find

I just can't figure out what the hell is wrong with me
Why this man of mine won't let us be
Love is evasive not to be in my life
You won't make me your one and only your wife

I go through life doing the best I can
Realizing it will never be enough for that man
I used to wake up optimistic thinking today's the day
When love and that man come and stay my way

Stop Lying To Me

Honesty is the best policy most people say
Unfortunately it doesn't seem very much to come my way
It appears it just something you just can't do
You continue to lie or omit things that's what you do

Am I so terrible you can't tell me the truth
When you lie to me I get mad and hit the roof
No matter you think you're protecting me
I just can't stand the lying can't you see

I have feelings sometimes I'm happy other times I hurt
Don't be inconsiderate and treat me like dirt
It's not what you do but how you do it to me
Lying just floors me it's an irritant don't you see

If you can't be totally honest with me
Then this thing just won't work out it can't be
You see if you lie or omit things to me
Then I'll never know the truth can't you see

Jealousy

I hate the jealous type and don't wanna be this way
It's a bad thing and just kind of ruins my day
I know you say I should trust in you
And believe in what you say too

But that old green-eyed monster creeps up over me
I get irrational cranky and mean as can be
It's a feeling I have little control over
Insecurity blows like a tornado roar

When you're not where you say you'll be
Those old doubts sneak up and worry me
I wear it like another face my green mask
I wonder how much more I can take how long can I last

It's a slow dripping poison like an IV to my heart
I know it's causing problems tearing us apart
I try and accept the reassurance I get from you
But jealously it's ugly it hurts oh yes it do

Kiss and Never Tell

You've told me over and over to never ever tell
So now I'm locked in my only private hell
I started this thing with my eyes open wide
This thing can't be acknowledged my feelings I must hide

Never mention my name is what you said to me
Cause it might get back to the one at home you see
No I can't let anyone know that we "the couple" exist
Can't let them see a special look or a kiss

When a woman loves a man she wants the world to know
Instead I have to deny it and say no no no
Can't even sit together or leave public places
No hint of recognition better cross my face

No we can't sit together side by side
My emotions I have to keep closed and hide
Dropping me off at the door just won't do
Mustn't drop any hints of the love between me and you

So I can kiss but better not tell
Wear the secret like a funeral veil
It's something I do to keep you in my life
Another battle to be fought and I'm losing the fight

Her She or Me

The game of love can get rough you see
So who's it gonna be *her she* or *me*
The competition wears me out at times
This man his love I can't seem to find

But four of us no one told me it would be like that
It gets to be tiring passé like an old hat
I never know who's winning who's in the lead
It's you and me one-on-one I need

My personality won't let me go out like that
It resists says no you can't do that
I just can't accept it don't want it to be true
I just base it on the things you say and do

Her, she's the one who's got you the best
Miles ahead of me a head above the rest
Then *She's* got something I don't seem to have
Exciting you making your heart laugh

Then there's Me bringing up the rear
The one with the most to fear
Mama didn't tell me it would times like this
Of the good things in a relationship like this I'd miss

The lonely nights I spend home alone in my bed
Sadly reflecting on the lies I've been fed
The hours I spend just waiting by the phone
Don't go anywhere just stay at home

The woman her, she shares your life
Cooking cleaning just like a wife
And *She* seems to always be around
Another conquest you've seem to have found

I don't quite know where I fit in all of this
I just know your love I've entirely missed
This kind of game I don't play so well
Locked up in my one private hell

What Have I Become

I never thought there would come a time in my life
I'd be the other woman to someone's woman or wife
It's a role I'm hardly suited to play
It becomes harder day after day

Stolen moments and stolen kisses telling no one
Sometimes it's a terrible burden little joy no fun
Sneaking around here and there
It's a terribly hard thing for me to bear

The lowest priority almost nothing in your life
It's stabs my heart feeling like it's pierced with a knife
Can't even call you on the telephone
The lonely days nights and weekends spent alone

Vacations we'll never take together we can't even share
I try to laugh it off and say I don't care
But to my inner self I am only lying
I just keep going at least keep on trying

What am I friend companion or mere lover
Knowing you really place no one above her
How or where do I fit into the scheme of things
Will I ever get the prize will I get the ring

Maybe you'll say the words I'm longing to hear
That I'm yours and yours alone my dear
I will be able to shout and tell the world you're mine
My life will be complete happy joyous and kind

My Joy and Pain

I awake sometimes in a warm hazy glow
In synch in rhythm just going with the flow
Knowing shortly it's you that I'll see
I say ' Thank You Lord' for sending him to me

I am lost inside a cozy world all my own
When you are with me I feel safe like being at home
But reality has a way of rearing its ugly head
My body feels heavy like a ton of lead

I remember you're not mine and I'm headed for a fall
You see I don't have a real love no not at all
No you belong to another someone else's man
I have to remember that I must I will I can

Yes another sleeps beside you at night
You turn to her for love and it doesn't seem right
My heart screams at the injustice of it all
I say love let it be me please hear my call

My joy and pain are one and the same
I saw I loved I ran I came
I pray for strength to get through this
Mine and only mine is my prayer and wish

In My Room

Away from the madness in the loneliness of my room
I fight desperately to keep away the doom and gloom
Sadness descends upon me like a thief in the night
It's so hard for me to distinguish wrong from right

Laying naked like a baby in the womb
Silence all around me like I'm enclosed in a tomb
Nothing but darkness encloses me
No sounds in the room but the breathing of me

My body tense and taut as I lie upon my bed
Thoughts running loose and rampant through my head
I lay here trying to make sense of my life
Pain courses through me with the sharpness of a knife

I can't seem to get it right get it together
Life's a long thunderstorm forever stormy weather
Sometimes I wonder if I should put an end to it all
As my emotions plummet then fall

Tears sometimes trickled down my face
My heart beats at an alarming pace
I sigh cry and let it all out
I rant, rave, holler and shout
Sleep puts me out of my misery to face yet another day
The nighttime blues in my room held temporarily at bay

Finally Letting Go

Finally after two years of...

arguments, tears, and praying the situation would change
I had to let go. Once again I was losing touch with me. It
became hard to distinguish reality. I didn't know if I was
coming or going. Talking to him didn't do a bit of good.
Life took a sort of surreal quality. He shut down
completely as far as we were concerned. I just didn't know
what to do. My dilemma was I wanted him to step to me
correctly even though the relationship started off on the
wrong foot. Two wrongs don't make a right.

In the back of my mind I wanted him to send her packing.
Not for me simply because he wanted to and it was the
right thing to do. But it was not to be. I was hurt as we
often are in love triangles. It's funny, I swore that I'd never
ever go that route and I guess that saying is true, 'never,
say, never'. Boy did those words come back to haunt me.
I guess I was naive or still buying into the fairy tale.

Love is a hurting thing. Eventually I learned the one
heals. It takes time and there is no limit of how long. I
didn't feel good about myself during that time frame. I

searched my heart and soul going through a lot of self-examinations. Trying to figure out where I went wrong.

It took a minute but finally I did heal. After a passage of time it didn't hurt so bad to say his name and listen to those love songs. Time heals all wounds even a bruised and broken heart.

When It's Over

When it's over I said I would know
That I'd had enough and it was time to go
I wouldn't hang on and prolong the agony
I would walk away my head held high you see

No I can't let him know he's hurting me so
It's over and we are no more
I want to scream yell holler and shout
Have a tantrum and just throw things about

Pain grips me like a vise squeezing my heart
Regardless the time has come for us to part
Cause in my head I know it's over
You my love choose to stay with her

I will take it one day at time
To fight off his heart stealing crime
I can't reminisce about how it used to be
Because I'll break down and go back to him you see

Even though it hurts I've got to be strong
To do all in my power to right this wrong
My prayer I chant all through the day
It's over and done and better this way

We're Through

My heart is heavy sadness etched upon my face
My eyes told you the truth I had to put you in your place
Every word I said was accurate and true
Still I hurt so bad I don't know what to do

I sit here with my head in my hands
Listening to you talk now you're my ex-man
I said Baby I've tried and I'm through
You said this thing you don't want to do

I'd been dreading that day for a very long time
Wearing myself out walking a thin line
You changed and I could no longer feel you
I got scared I didn't know what to say or do

I wanted to say I changed my mind I want you to stay
But I knew you'd never see things my way
We been through this a time or two before
You wanted less and I wanted more

I've got to face it yes we're really through
If only we could go back to when feelings were new
God can it really be true
That you and I yes we're through

Healing

One day this hurt and sorrow will end
My heart will get stronger yes it will mend
Tears will cease to fill the corners of my eyes
I will kiss heartache and sorrow goodbye

One day there will be joy and no pain
There's a love out there for me soon to be gained
I will feel free as a bird soaring through the air
The wind will whisper and kiss my hair

One day I won't feel this bad anymore
I'll find the courage to walk through that open door
Taking a giant step to better my life
Free it of all sadness sorrow and strife

One day I won't have to wonder what I did wrong
I will be singing a new tune and different song
There will be a new bounce in my step
I'll rise to the occasion the challenge will be met

There's nothing better in the world then peace of mind
I got the message and I read your signs
Yes these old burdens will be gone away
It will be a beautiful and wonderful day

Time Goes On

I like a fool believed in you
And all the things you said we would do
This man he walked in and changed my life
I was to be all things to you woman lover and wife

Time has a way of just stepping in
Making you realize sometimes you just can't win
He couldn't be my lover and certainly not my friend
It's time to let it go just let it end

You said yes but reality was no
And it hurt badly and wounded me so
I tried hard to remain true in my heart
Instead the time has come for us to part

Love is a give and take they say
I kept waiting patiently for the day
When you became mine and we became one
But times went on and we became none

I wanted to believe in what you said
To be happy joyous uplifted and gay
But the passing time got in the way
It just became a continuation of the previous day

Afterthoughts

Everyone has the right to decide the best course to take regarding one's personal life. It's not something you can advise anyone. Everybody has their own destiny to follow, their own life to lead. I think some of us think we can change their minds and sometimes it's just the challenge. For others, it's just a preference. Believe it not, there are those of us who just plain love the man. The good thing is that we can change our minds. Healing the heart is a little harder than changing one's mind, it takes time and a lot of courage, but like I said- it can eventually be done.

The Diary or Just Another Way of Saying The Same Old Thing...

Well how did you like my story in verse form? I hope you

didn't think I stopped there, not me! I also kept a journal

or diary detailing the relationship. I called my diary *Di*,

(get it)? So why don't you take a peek at the following

pages. I don't mind sharing, at least not this time. We've

come this far let's not stop now, you see it's,

Just Another Way Of Saying The Same Old Thing!

May 1

I swear cross my heart and hope to die (not!) that today is 'THE DAY' girlfriend. (I know you're just a book of sorts a diary, hence the name Di). I am going to break up with Curtis. Kick his butt to the curb over and out. I've given that man way too much of my time and infinite chances to do the right thing. I knew he was trouble the minute he laid those big ole green eyes on me. Let's not forget those dimples looking like packed ice cream carved with a spoon. It's time for this Sistah to insist he put up or shut-up. Step up to the plate. Curtis has to opportunity to score a home run or just plain strike out.

I've been divorced for two and a half years. My relationship with Gerry shut me down. When I say down I mean as low as a basset hound's stomach. I had lost that integral part of me. Are you feeling me? You know the woman part of me. I didn't feel any emotion and didn't even question why I felt that way. I was convinced my lot in life was to exist in a lonely environment.

The only satisfaction or pleasure I felt in my life was when it applied to my sons or my job. I didn't feel desirable or feel desire for a man. I tried hard to continue that way of life, I really did. I kept up the charade for the last six of fourteen years of marriage.

Why, you ask? I felt I had to hang in there for our sons, Mykal, age fifteen and Gerald Jr. twelve years old at the time of our divorce. Our game plan was to perpetrate the myth until Gerry Jr. turned eighteen. We all gave stellar performances to all on the outside looking in. Hell we all could have won Academy Awards.

My boys look like me but in different ways. Mykal and Gerry Jr. are handsome young men, tall, dark, chocolate males with slim physiques. Like I was back in my day. My sons are polite, sensitive, helpful and well-mannered young men.

Between Gerry and myself we've tried to instill in our sons the importance of having goals in life. As time goes on we'll see what life has in store for them. I am quite proud of my boys and as I stated they give me a reason for living.

Mykal and Gerry Jr. were very supportive of the divorce both being old enough to sense things were not quite right in the Walters household. A rash of deaths brought me out of my comatose state long enough to realize that tomorrow is not promised. The time had come for me to move on with my life. Di I had lost me. The Marissa Walters of old was dead and gone.

Our sons were the best part of the marriage. We were better parents than spouses. I worry though how our ill-fated marriage will affect their future relationships. I feel we were such lousy role models. Thank God Di my

47

divorce wasn't because of Curtis or any other man. Had that been the case I would be crazy or insane right about now.

Gerry and I hadn't shared a bedroom, much less a bed for at least three years. After I fessed up that tidbit to my closest friends, they told me I was crazy. How the hell did I go without *IT* for so many years was all I'd heard from them. They told me that was just plain unnatural. I tried to explain when you lose yourself other aspects go along with it. Not to mention I learned very well how to satisfy my own needs when I had the itch. Hindsight is 20/20 they say. I am a slow learner but I am getting there slowly but surely.

So today Di May first I am going to be strong. I will not weaken. I'll give you the 411 tonight. You'll see I'll pull it off. There is no doubt in my mind (well maybe a little). I haven't kept a journal or diary for a while. I will document the rise or fall of Curtis and Marissa.

Well Di I hate to admit it but I weakened. Curtis got to me again. His puppy dog eyes glistened with just the right touch of moisture. He hugged me tightly and told me he was not letting me go.

"No Rissa" he pleaded, "not yet Baby. You can't just write us off. I'm going to do right by you I swear. I know you've been hurt in the past. You know we belong to each other. Just one week. Baby please just give me one week. Seven days."

The upshot is that Curtis has exactly one week to remove Retha his live-in lover from his house. This was the closest he'd come to an actual commitment. Being the foolish romantic that I am I agreed. Did I mention Curtis and I work together Di? How's that for a messy situation. Well got to run now. I want to see my boys before they head off with Gerry for the weekend.

Bit by bit you crept into my heart
We were meant to be forever never apart
You see I'd given up on love so long ago
Loneliness had become my enemy, my foe

May 2

The shrill ring of the telephone penetrated my dark shroud of sleep. Curtis aka my dll (down low lover) was on the line. How he hates me calling him that.

"Whassup Rissa?" He asked cheerfully, as if it wasn't the wee hours of five o'clock in the morning.

"You got it," I replied. On second thought *no he doesn't. Not really.* Di he doesn't have a darn thing. I'm here alone in this big ole bed and he's home. "Did you talk to Retha?" I asked. The words burst from my mouth like a speeding bullet before I could catch myself.

"Let's just say I broached the subject. Yeah baby I put it out there." He bragged.

"What do you mean?" I asked confused wide-awake by then. There was no fogginess as my mind segued to crystal clear alertness.

"I'm sowing the seeds." He whispered.

I could hear his name called in the background. Curtis usually calls me from the basement of his house. He has his own telephone line and Retha hers. "I'll call you later." He promised.

With that said all that was left was the bong-bong of the dial tone in my ear. In the past I would have been overjoyed that he'd called. Now all I felt was tired. It was going to be a long day and he'd jumpstarted it before I was ready.

Oh well. I hopped out of bed and hurried to the shower after deciding to treat myself to breakfast. I was back home in an hour. Di I absolutely loathe weekends. That's when loneliness hits me like a ton of bricks. Curtis and I almost never see each other over the weekends. He calls more than he does during the week. But like the song goes 'Ain't Nothing Like The Real Thing'. And more times than not I feel dissatisfied after his calls.

I decided to get my hair done today instead of tomorrow and do a little grocery shopping maybe hit the bookstore hmmm.... With the boys at their father's for the weekend and dll out of commission I felt depressed.

Several hours later I was back home in the bed and asleep before you could say abracadabra. I tried paging Curtis. No response

Di I must never ever call him at home only page him. I've called him exactly once since we started dating. Maybe a minute after we hung up I decided to take the plunge and call him back. You guessed Di Retha answered the phone. I disguised my voice but Sistah girl seemed suspicious and I pretended to be a friend of Curtis' daughter.

The things we do when the one we choose isn't available. As the day progressed I watched a little television and read a book. Later I fixed myself dinner then ate. Drank a little wine watched a little television and drank a little more wine and that was all she wrote.

May 3

Let's see Di what else do I need to tell you about my love situation and myself? I've already mentioned Curtis and I work for the same company. We're both in the Information Technology field employed by a large manufacturing company. Being in the IT field translates to lots of off-hour work and the perfect opportunity to spend what we define as quality time together. Sometimes it just feels like a damn nightmare. On the plus side we do get to travel together more about that later.

The telephone rang and penetrated my hazy cloak of sleep. My reactions were just a little bit slow. The wine had helped chase my demons away last night. I groped for the phone and croaked, "Hello?" All the while praying fingers and toes crossed it was Curtis.

But alas it was not to be. Instead my job needed a little Sunday morning expertise from moi. Thirty minutes later the problem was resolved and back to dreamland for me. I woke up around ten thirty my head aching just a bit. I have way too much time on my hands today. I should have left a few chores or errands to do today.

I became a member of the big 40 club this past March. I have been described as a nice looking woman. I am 5'10 inches tall with honey brown colored skin. I weigh about 170 pounds that I carry well or so I've been told. I wear my hair in the ever-popular Toni Braxton/Halle Berry haircut.

My hair texture is thin. I was cursed with the stuff that drops at the first touch of a strong wind. My sons inherited the hair curse and keep theirs cropped short. Mykal went through a phase where he experimented with a ponytail. As the old folks say I spit them out. Mykal is still growing and tops off around 6 feet tall. Gerry Jr. recently experienced a growth spurt so now I look up to both my sons. They are both two fine brothers if I may say so myself. I admit though there is some prejudice.

I married Gerald Sr. when I was twenty-three years old. Mykal was two years old and the product of a previous relationship. Six years and Gerry Jr. into the marriage I knew I'd made a mistake. Ours was pretty much a case of opposites attract. The opposition was too strong for us to overcome. We maintained it was better for the boys to have both parents rather than end up a statistic.

Unfortunately that is what I caused them to become. As part of the divorce decree I received half of the house, a beautiful tan colored split-level structure. You know it's funny Gerry and the boys really loved the place we called home. It just wasn't my first choice. So between my salary and child support I do okay. Not enough for the many extras growing boys need but I manage to keep a roof over our heads and food in the freezer. Enough already. The story of Gerald and Marissa Walters is another volume of journals altogether.

So Di question is do I leave the house? What if Curtis calls? I feel stir crazy maybe I'll run to the mall for a minute. I need to kill some time, later girl...

The lonely nights I spend alone in my bed
Reflecting on the lies I've been fed
The hours I spend waiting by the telephone

Don't go anywhere stay at home

May 4

My eyes flew open like a window shade opened to let the sunshine in. I awakened as usual five minutes before my alarm clock signaled the onset of the day. I'm one of those people with their own internal clock and I do believe in the saying the early bird catches the worm. I'm going to catch mine and then some. It's Monday and Di and I'll see Curtis in approximately four hours. Being the efficient not to mention effective person that I am, my clothes were ironed and ready to don. Did I mention Di the importance of clothes at the workplace, particularly when your dll works there also? Yes, I dress to please and this morning was no exception. The battle lines had been drawn between Retha and myself.

At six o'clock sharp I sat in my office logging onto the system. Curtis puts in an appearance around seven thirty. That gives me time to check the status of the network as well as respond to voice and emails. I also assist operations/network if needed. At seven forty five my telephone rang it was Curtis with queries. How was I this morning? Did I do anything over the weekend (translation did I meet any available men)? That was the sum of our usual Monday morning chitchat. He was impatience to see him some Rissa. I told him give me a minute and I'd meet him in the canteen.

I glided down the hall like a figure skater on ice. Anticipation had been making me wait. I felt a smile tug at the corner of my mouth as I sat across from Curtis. He gave me that look that told me I had it going on. Di my choice of clothing was definitely a winner. Oops I forgot to mention Retha works for the same company. No not in our building, I'm not that bold. Give me a little credit. She works at corporate headquarters a couple of suburbs north of the data center. Talk about a love triangle.

The morning flew by. It was lunchtime, eleven thirty one of my favorite times of the day. Three o'clock when I'm done for the day is the best especially paydays. Before I could put my phone on voice mail it rang. *Damn* I thought, *here we go.*

Curtis voice boomed into my ear. "Rissa, I hate to do this but I've got to pass on lunch."

I twisted the telephone cord and asked quietly, "what's up?"

"Retha's on her way here. She wants to talk and decided to meet me for lunch.

I saw red. They reside in the same house and couldn't talk there. "Excuse me." I said in my iciest tone, "are you telling me you're having lunch with the same woman you said would be out of your house in a week?"

55

His replied in an equally cold tone, "Rissa we'll talk later. Let's meet after work. I have something to show you."

I laid the phone down gently. Had I been home his ear would be ringing right about now. I was not a happy camper Di. I couldn't believe what I'd just heard. He gives her an ultimatum and she meets him for lunch. Something is wrong in Dodge. What's a woman to do?

I picked up a tuna sandwich and parked in our favorite spot where I did a perfect imitation of *Sistah with An Attitude*. The remainder of the afternoon passed quickly. I began preparing to leave for the day. As I powered down my pc who came slinking into my office? You guessed Curtis.

"Sorry about lunch," he mumbled as he slid into my extra chair. "You know I couldn't help it. I'm trying to break it off cleanly. I don't want her to even think there's another woman involved or she'll never leave."

Now Di I'm of the mind if you want something done follow Nike's lead, hell just do it. So if he tells her its time to go sistah should just commence to packing. Adios, Goodbye, See ya!

"Please bear with me a few more days," he pleaded.

My anger melted like butter in a hot skillet. Curtis knows which buttons to push and push them he does quite well. I calmed down. I tried to keep the whining out of my voice unsuccessfully. "So Mr. Lewis are we still on to meet after work?"

He replied smiling as he stood. "Of course. See you at four o'clock."

I left work with far less attitude, than when I went to lunch. I drove up the street to another hideaway then pulled out my cell phone and called home. I morphed into drill sergeant mode. Gerry Jr. answered the telephone and I questioned him relentlessly. "Where is Mykal? Is he at work? Is your homework done? I'll be home in about an hour." I also warned him for the millionth time how loud music causes hearing loss.

I'd told Mykal and Gerry Jr. those same words at least a million times. My utterances fell on deaf ears. I scolded Gerry Jr., "turn down the music, it's entirely too loud." On the plus side I know their lingo pretty good and thought I'd never admit it to them I like some rap artists.

Gerry asked, "What's for dinner? Are you cooking or are we having fast food?"

That's their first choice always. I finished the call with the news he never wants to hear, "Sorry son, I'm cooking."

I was deep into a chapter of my book when Curtis pulled up. Before he could ask my place or yours (translation your car or mine) his cell phone went off. Charles planned to attend a function at school this

evening and forgot to mention his plans to Curtis earlier.
He called to verify Curtis was on his way home so he
could use the car.

Our time as many times before was cut short. We
talked for a few minutes and then I asked him what he had
to show me.

"Tomorrow baby you can't see it until then."

I insisted, "I want to see it now" But he wasn't having
it. "Come on Curtis," I said changing tactics, kissing and
blowing gently into his ear, "Tell me what it is?"

He shook his head from side to side. "We don't
have time now. But I promise you that you're going to like
it."

I gave up seeing as how putting the moves on him was
not working. We said our farewells kissed, hugged and
set off in opposite directions. I arrived home half an hour
later. I fixed dinner and caught up on the day's
happenings with the boys. Then it was time to enter my
lonely bedroom.

I paged Curtis no response. When he and I started
dating he'd call me every night. He said my voice was the
last one he wanted to hear before going to sleep. Di
times have truly changed.

May 5

After I arrived at work there was yet another fire to be doused courtesy of the Operations Department. I decided to call my Momma. When I was a little girl I thought my Momma was the bomb. She is greatly admired by all, a churchgoing woman who raised four daughters on her own. She is pretty innovative too. Daddy died when I was fifteen years old. Not wanting to leave us girls home alone she started catering from our kitchen and sewing. Sort of home based businesses back in the day. Thank God she was blessed with marketable skills many women of her generation were not as fortunate.

I am the oldest followed by Adele, Deanna, and Corrine. Adele is four years younger than me and she is two years older than Deanna. Deanna is three years older than Corrine. Our family is unique. I was adopted courtesy of a family member and Deanna was a foster child. She became a member of our family when she was eight years old. We were raised and taught that we were 'full-bloodied sisters'.

Di it pains me to write this but something went awry along the way. My sisters and I are just not close. Something is wrong. I've spent many days, months, and years pondering WHY. I can't figure it out. We don't really communicate at least not on a personal level. I don't know if it's me or if there's a personality conflict. You know what I really don't know how they feel about Deanna and me. I love my sisters all of them being fortunate enough to grow up with both biological and adopted ones.

Neither Corrine nor Adele, have ever asked Deanna or myself how we feel regarding our birth situations. Perhaps it's just me being nosy. I guess this inquiring mind would want to know.

Both Deanna and I share relationships with our biological mothers. As we try to better understand the circumstances that brought us to Martha Bailey. We have our place in each other's lives. Don't get me wrong. I truly don't understand why our relationship is like that.

I am fed surface information regarding my sister's lives. Deanna and I don't share personal information with Corrine and Adele. Maybe it's me being too sensitive and there's just not any.

We don't deal with adversity well as a family mainly because we don't really discuss issues. The biggest bombshell to hit our family at least that I am aware of was my divorce. I called my family members individually and explained the situation. When I told my sister Adele she cried like a baby. I became so irritated that I got off the telephone ten minutes into the conversation. I told her I needed her to be there for me and after she got herself together to call me back.

Corrine suggested Gerry and I talk to someone and get counseling. She works at a hospital and could put me in touch a professional. I told her we didn't love each other. At least I no longer loved him. The divorce was a done deal so counseling was out.

Only Deanna was supportive, but at the time she was having marital problems of her own. Di I don't understand it. They're my family and I receive very little from them by way of emotional support. I didn't want a pity party. But I was hoping to hear 'we love you and if you need someone to talk to I'm here for you'. I guess that was wistful thinking on my part.

Momma was supportive in her way, though I felt she disapproved. At least she gave me the benefit of the doubt. Di I wish things were different with my sisters. I know Adele and Corrine are close. Those two are like two peas in a pod. I really envy their relationship. I wish I had a sister I could turn to in times of trouble.

I've talked with my friend Pam about my sister issue. She wisely told me talking to my sisters about our relationship is a demon that I'll have to face one day. I'll know when the time was right. I've talked to Gerry about my feelings many times. His explanation as well as Momma's was my sisters love me. My ex and momma didn't see a problem.

Curtis and I had a few conversations on the subject. He bluntly told me, that it comes back to bloodlines. He inferred I was in denial and a smart woman. I'd figure it out when I'm ready to go there.

Problem is I'm just not ready just yet. God willing one day I will be. Sorry Di I do digress.

I called Momma. She asked how the boys and I were doing. Momma said my sisters and their families were doing fine. The Memorial Day holiday is looming over the horizon and Corrine and Sam are hosting the family gathering. My youngest sister would call me and give me my food assignment.

Twenty minutes later the conversation ended. I sighed audibly, not really feeling up to a family outing. My family knows of Curtis. But haven't met him. The Bailey family was chomping at the bit to do so. Of course they were unaware of his living arrangement. I hadn't really discussed our relationship with anyone other than my friend Sharon at work. She instructed me to be careful and she was there for me if I needed her.

My family celebrates each and every holiday together and dinner is always late. Momma says there is always one late person in a family and that we must accept everyone as they are. Problem with potluck is you can't eat until all the food has been delivered to the family hosting the event. I know Di it's all good and I realize some families never celebrate together. Still since we do potluck, we'll never, ever in this lifetime have dinner on time. It kind of makes it difficult to visit friends or other relatives because we always gather together – the family first rule.

No one not one sister including myself has ever cooked a meal solo. One thing I'll say about my ex-mother-in-law is whenever she hosted the holidays I never had to bring anything. Don't get me wrong I'd offer and she'd just say bring yourself. Her way of doing things was totally different from my own family and it took me a while to get used to the concept. And yes, Mother Patton's dinners always began on time.

My boys are into the family thing also. One Christmas the boys were afflicted with chicken pox and I tried hard to make the holiday special. I cooked even baked a couple of cakes. (Di I hate baking with a passion too time consuming). I bought extra gifts, the whole nine yards. They complained the entire day. Needless to say that was the first and only holiday the four of us shared without the extended family.

Since Curtis and I started dating holidays have become a drag. We have yet to celebrate one together. We go around and around the subject with no resolution in sight. He did promise me we'd go see Momma next week so they'll finally meet. Talking to Momma is depressing sometimes it's a subtle reminder of the state of sisterhood.

Enough already. Let me get back to work. My fingers are crossed that today will be a good one. My workday is done and I still didn't know what Curtis had to show me. Cest la vie.

I thought not doing things together wouldn't bother me
I lied to myself big time denial I didn't want to see
The simple things most couples take for granted
A phone call, drinks going out for dinner and dancing

May 6

I awakened bright and early as usual. I actually wore a suit to work today. In my department there are jokes when you wear a suit. A good indication one could be looking for another job. So I knew I would hear it from my team. I am giving a presentation this morning and afternoon demonstrating hardware I support.

I am a software specialist. Bet you don't know what that is? I install communications software that allows companies to access each other's mainframes or computers. I also support hardware relating to communications. Curtis is a hardware specialist. His job entails installing modems, telephone lines, routers and dsus. He has jokes about my software and his hardware merging. It's true though you can't have one without the other.

I also prepare and teach classes on some of the software I support for the network group. Today I am ready to just get the task over and done with. I tend to get a little nervous speaking in front of a group. I stopped by Curtis's office but he wasn't there. I was disappointed. Come to think of it a lot about the relationship bothers me lately.

I thought I had it going on clad in my navy blue suit, with matching pumps, a white silk blouse, and hosiery. My ears twinkled like stars. I wore a pair of diamond earrings Curtis had given me for my birthday. I guess it's a guy thing. Curtis wanted to erase all traces of Gerry. To date he's replaced a good chunk of my jewelry and bought me a Dooney and Burke bag with matching accessories as well as clothing.

After entering the conference room, I proceeded to distribute my handouts. The attendees began pouring into the room and before long I started. Who comes strolling in late? You guessed Curtis. I gave him a quizzical look as if to say what are you doing here? In response he winked. Sistah needs her job not to mention the benjamins. So I was at my professional best. An hour and a half later I was done. My mission accomplished it was a wrap. Curtis helped me gather the extra handouts, stacking them up neatly for the afternoon session. He strategically bumped into me a couple of times. I asked, "What are you doing here?"

He answered wickedly as he leered at me, "Just call me Mr. Moral Support."

I beamed.

He leaned towards me and added, "Lunch 1130? The Chinese restaurant?"

I stared at him bemused with my arms folded across my chest and answered I'd be there.

Lunch should have been fine. Di for some reason nothing in this relationship ever comes easy. I noticed Debra one of our co-workers seated across the room. I am aware that she had a crush on Curtis. Debra is about ten years younger than us. Curtis is two years older than me.

I toward him and asked softly, "I wonder what she's doing here?"

He replied innocently, as he spread his napkin in his lap, "I don't have a clue."

We go to many out-of-the way restaurants near the job in order to avoid running into someone who may know Retha.

"Do you think we should go over and speak to her?" he asked nonchalantly teasing me.

I replied with a deadpan expression, "I think waving is sufficient."

Periodically she'd stare at our table. No let me correct that statement. Sistah salivated hungrily at Curtis like he was the main course. She's in his office more often than I like. I've asked many times what they talk about. What does she want from him? He tells me she's like a little sister. She asks him for advice. He says she has a boyfriend. (I doubt that).

We waved to her in perfect synchronization. Her presence killed the mood for me. Let me explain why. Curtis and I usually share a breakfast break and lunch unless we are in team player mode. We either meet after work or take an afternoon break together before I leave for the day. Six months ago Curtis broke our lunch date for no apparent reason. In fact he was very vague about the whole thing. I left for lunch after deliberating if I wanted to dine in a restaurant or pick-up fast food and eat in the car.

Dining in won hands down. I decided to go to a restaurant about three miles from work. I walked in the restaurant and the waitress seated me. I placed my order and opened my book. I look up and whom do I see? Curtis and Debra. I did a double take and I'm sure my mouth gaped like a fish out of water. I decided to be cool even though I was furious. I finished my first course, soup and emitted a little burp. I was determined I was not going to look in their direction.

Suddenly there was a voice in my ear. Curtis whispered, "some people you just can't take anywhere."

I looked up and he stood behind me, smiling like he didn't have a care in the world.

I told him after I uncovered my mouth. "That may be the case. But obviously you don't have a problem taking other people to lunch with you." I had to catch myself before the words I'd heard so many times before passed from my lips what if Retha walks in?

I swear Di this man has me doing and saying things I wouldn't ordinarily. I was hot and was sure my face was flushed.

Feeling hurt, I told him that I wished he'd told me that he was having lunch with Debra. First Curtis teased me and kept saying I was jealous. Then it dawned on him that I was really mad. He tried to reassure me nothing was going on between them. But I wasn't having it. They departed before I did.

Debra gave me a phony little wave as they left. I was not in the best of moods the remainder of the day. Mercifully time flew by. I was home by three thirty. The boys cheered me up, regaling me with tales of their day. No phone call tonight and no Di I didn't page him.

Trust is such a small little five-letter word
Sometimes vague and subtle, like a soaring bird
Trust should be easy, yet I find it so hard

It's elusive to me like finding a lucky card

May 7

When I arrived at work this morning a red rose was placed strategically on my desk. Lying next to the flower was an unsigned card simply stating 'I'm Sorry.' I figured Curtis must have left it the day before. I began my daily network check when my telephone rang. It was my sister Corrine. I remembered Momma telling me she'd call. This was a first because Corrine isn't usually so proactive. She tends to do things at the last minute. I figured she must have a hidden agenda his name Curtis.

We exchanged pleasantries inquiring about each other's children's health and progress in school. Corrine is the sister I talk to the least. We converse by telephone maybe four or five times a year. She asked what I wanted to bring for the holiday.

I told her, "Just tell me what you want me to brigand I'll do that." We settled on spaghetti and a case of pop.

Then the real reason she called became apparent. "Will Curtis and his children be attending the barbeque?" she asked innocently.

I answered quickly, "I'll let you know later."

She went on to add, "It would be nice to meet the man who has so captivated my big sister."

I could have gagged. We chatted a little longer and then thank God the conversation ended. I walked down the hall towards the canteen area. The time was about seven twenty five a.m. I glanced out of the window to see if Curtis had arrived at work. Who do I see walking together? You guessed Curtis and Debra. *Damn. She swarms around him like a fly at a picnic table.*

I walked back to my office. I didn't like this one bit. I love Curtis deeply. He awakened feelings physically and mentally in me. Curtis was my equal maybe even my soul mate. I am usually optimistic that we'll make it to the next level of our relationship. But another woman was too much for even me. We have our ups and downs still I feel in the end our love would prevail.

Curtis and I were friends before we became lovers. We didn't really mess around too heavy before my divorce, No sex was my rule until I was single and free. A little while later with a phony smile on my face I walked down to the canteen for our morning rendezvous. Curtis joined me a few minutes later.

A smile lighting his face, "Just call me Your Dunkin Donut Man," he joked. It was his morning to pick up breakfast.

I could see love and affection in his eyes. He touched my hair and complemented me on my attire. I asked how things were coming with Retha. He sighed looked down and replied, "She's adjusting to the idea.

We talked at lunch and again last night. I'm sorry I didn't call you last night. I just don't want to give her any opportunities to give me trouble over this. Rissa, I do want us to be together. Just bear with me Baby and hang in there." He pushed a batch of papers across the table.

At the same time my pager went off, I glanced at them and told him, "Later duty calls." I asked, "Eleven thirty?"

May 8

Di I was really busy yesterday and didn't get a chance to get back to you. We experienced a system outage at work. When that happens the shop turns in a beehive of activity. I was one tired sistah when I arrived home. Nestled in the batch of papers Curtis gave me was an eviction notice. The first item that caught my eye was the date, June first. The deadline expired today.

Curtis and I had a serious argument when he called. He tried to justify his decision. For example, Retha needed more time to find an apartment as well as get her finances together. He went on to say she was there for him when he had nothing. Surely he could give her more time. He said I was being unreasonable and that's when I lost it. I slammed the telephone into the cradle.

I should probably give you some background on Curtis' wife Gail and Ms. Retha. Gail battled alcoholism unsuccessfully it caused the demise of their marriage. After the divorce she was left with half the house, furniture, car and full custody of children. A few years later, Curtis managed to buy out of her half of the house and regain custody of their son Charles and daughter Christine.

He was very bitter about the divorce, her alcoholism and not being able to see his children when he wanted. Curtis didn't work at the data center when all that drama occurred so I never saw that side of him. Not too long after he regained all that was near and dear to him and Gail moved out of Illinois.

Charles is a year older than Mykal and Christine a year older than Gerry. Retha the ink barely dry on her own divorce decree being the good friend she was helped a brother out. She invited Curtis to share her living space. The stay was to be temporary until he got back on his feet. She ended up losing her house shortly after Cutis moved back home. She was to stay with him for a couple of weeks. Day turned into weeks and weeks into months. They have been together for eleven years. Retha has time on her side. There's something between them no matter how Curtis denies it.

I can't imagine staying with someone if there were no feelings involved. I guess that's kind of like the pot calling the kettle black since that's what I did with Gerry. The difference in my mind is that we were married not just living together.

At some point in time Curtis and Gail, Retha and her ex resided in the same the same apartment complex. My theory is they were messing around even then. Hell in some states she's his common- law wife. Let me give you the 411 on Ms. Retha. She married early at eighteen or nineteen years of age.

She is the mother of four children. Her ex husband has custody of their youngest child Latanya. She's fourteen years old. Retha's two oldest daughters are adults with children. Her only son is incarcerated. Latanya stays at Curtis' house every other weekend, like Gerry and my boys. Curtis and Latanya do not get along at all. Christine is not crazy about her either. It makes me wonder how we'll interact, if by some miracle we manage to reside together. Will we all just get along?

I tease Curtis about being a grandfather. He doesn't find my remarks amusing. Yes I've seen Ms. Retha before, just not up close and personal. One must check out the competition. Curtis brought pictures of her to work to appease my curiosity. Hell I even know the color and type of car she drives. Sorry I didn't memorize her license plate number. I'm not that anal.

One afternoon very early in our relationship, I was driving home from work and she was obviously on her way to meet him. I glanced in the car, no our eyes didn't meet. I had only a side view of her. She's an attractive, short light brown skinned, shapely woman. She doesn't wear her hair in any particular style according to Curtis. He claims she's a sloppy housekeeper. Her hair is a mess and she just plain let herself go. That's one of the things he claims to like about me how I manage to keep it all together. That can either be a blessing or a curse. Does that imply that I must always look my best?

To be honest, I don't fear Retha as an object of his affection. I know he cares for me but possession is nine tenths of the law. He claims she has a temper and can get physical at times. Little does brother know I can go a few rounds myself. We just haven't been put to the test.

Curtis is about my height and a little on the chubby side. His complexion is reddish brown or redbone as they called it back in the day. He has green or hazel eyes depending on his mood. His brown hair is closely cropped. The only sign of age are speckles of gray in his beard and moustache. He says he's just an average guy in the looks department. I realize my hopes may never come to fruition. I'll be patient for now. I'm out. Thank God it's Friday!

Maybe just maybe you'll say the words
I'm longing to hear
That I'm yours and yours alone my dear

74

I will be able to shout and tell the world you're mind
My life will be complete joyous and kind

May 9

It's Mother's Day Weekend. I cleaned the house,
did grocery shopping and ran miscellaneous errands.
The boys decided to sleep over at a friend's house
tonight so boredom set in quickly once they left. I
decided to make a Barnes and Noble run. I love books
and could spend hours walking up and down the aisles.
My last stop on the way back home was the grocery
store. I had a taste for a nice juicy steak for dinner. I was
home by three o'clock.

I thought for a hot second maybe I'd run to the city
and see Momma. The books won out in the end and I
decided to stay home and indulge myself in my favorite
pastime.

My sister Adele called to say hey! We talked for a
little while. She asked about my Mother's Day plans.
Then she coyly asked if I was coming to the city.

I told her I doubted it and all I wanted for Mother's
Day was to stay home. My dream was to be waited on
hand and foot and watch basketball. I could sense her
disapproval. I'm sure she felt I should spend the day with
the family. I'd already sent Momma a floral basket. It's

scheduled to be delivered tomorrow. Mama sent me a card and it arrived in the mail a week ago.

I admit Di I am selfish but I put in some heavy-duty hours at work. I get telephone calls in the middle of the night. I've even had to work while on vacation. My career is strewn with stress.

During my last physical my doctor urged me to consider changing jobs. I told her not yet that I'd consider it when the right opportunity presented itself. Let's not forget Curtis is there and you know how that is. Adele and I talked a few more minutes, then back to the book for me. I dozed off.

The telephone rang again. Gerry Jr. said gregariously. "Whassup Mom? I'm just calling to check on you."

I told him all was well. "I'm just chillin – sitting with a book."

We talked about his activities that day. Then back into the recesses of my dreams I went. Trying hard to reach a place where no one could hurt me. The telephone rang once again. *Damn! It's like Union Station around here. I can't get any sleep.*

I picked up the receiver. It was Curtis. He was scheduled to go to work at three o'clock tomorrow morning. What did I think about joining him?

Since I only live thirteen miles from the job I informed him it was doable. I suggested he come to my house when he finished work instead of me coming there. I'd have breakfast waiting.

He declined stating the long drive would tire him out and he wanted me to come there. I broiled myself that steak for dinner. Later I set my alarm clock for two o'clock am.

May 10

Di I'm surprised I got any sleep at all. I woke up around one thirty and slipped on blue jeans and an orange tee shirt. I headed out the door rushing like a jackrabbit fleeing its lair. I like driving late at night and early in the morning. It's so peaceful. There's no traffic just darkness surrounding me like dotted navy blue velvet. I stopped at Dunkin Donut the only place open that time of the morning.

I arrived at the building in no time and walked down the hallway to Curtis' office. I could hear the peck, peck of his typing. I gave him a kiss and sat down and read while he completed his work. Three hours later he was done. He asked if I was up for breakfast. I told him the offer still stood. I could cook us a meal at my house. I made up my mind to be cool if he didn't come.

After breakfast we went to the duck pond. Cutis had a surprise for me. You know Di my mind was in the gutter. It's not like we hadn't ever made out in our vehicles

77

before. Instead he pulled a Victoria Secrets bag out of the trunk of his car. I tore into it like a child on Christmas morning. It was gold nightwear a little slip of a thing. I thanked him showering kisses on his face. He reminded me that he wouldn't be able to spend the day with me. I'd be in his thoughts and he would try to call me during the day.

We parted thirty minutes later. I was back home in my bed shortly. I'm sure there was a smile on my face as I slept. The boys returned home at noon. They had gifts too. Mykal informed me, they had enough money to treat me to dinner or we could stay home and watch the basketball game. I opted for the game. They went into the kitchen to prepare their specialty Chicken Alfredo courtesy of Chicken Helper. I called Momma and my sisters. The boys and I ate dinner and then watched the game. It was a very good day indeed, Di.

Just say the work and I'll come to you
This love is everlasting, glorious and true
I'll be there for you, a promise I keep
Feelings run so long and so very deep

May 11

Di I was in a quiet mood this morning. Curtis was tied up working on a problem. Since he couldn't meet me for breakfast I went to the smoker's room instead. I admit that I indulge in that filthy habit as the general public has described it. I sighed as I put out my cigarette. Though deep in thought I sensed someone invading my space.

I looked up as Eddie Curtis' best buddy sat next to me. "How are you this morning, Marissa?" he asked.

I nodded my head. "Fine."

I was not in the mood for Eddie antics this morning. He's a tall, heavyset pecan colored man with the biggest hands I've ever seen. I have to admit I've wondered if that saying was true? Hand and foot size...hmm.

"So how is our boy this morning?" he inquired?

I shook my head from side to side and replied, "I don't know Eddie. I haven't seen him this morning."

We chatted about mutual projects. I glanced at my watch hoping to make a graceful exit. But before I could stand and get the hell out of Dodge, Eddie went there. To that place I feared. I knew what was coming.

"Marissa," he began bluntly, "I know you either love or have strong feelings for Curtis. He's my boy and all. But he is incapable of love."

If I had been a white woman, I'm sure my face would have been beet red. "Eddie this is not the time or place for this," I retorted heatedly. Luckily we were the only ones in the room.

"Come on," he continued, "I don't think there will ever be a right time or place as far as you're concerned.

79

Marissa. You just don't want to hear what I have to say. You know Gail hurt him badly and until he Curtis resolves those issues, he will never be able to love anyone. I like you very much. You are a beautiful, intelligent woman. You're just getting out of a bad situation yourself. I just don't want to see you get hurt and or have unrealistic expectations."

Eddie is fifteen years older than Curtis and myself. He sees himself as a father/brother figure to Curtis. I found this whole situation hypocritical, because I know for a fact Eddie was cheating on his own wife. Hmm. *You probably taught him too well.*

Eddie continued, "Gail was his first love. He trusted her implicitly and she let him down. I feel you have a huge capacity for love. Just make sure you're giving your love to the right man. Open your eyes and see this thing for what it is and not what you want it to be."

By this time I was halfway at the door. "Thanks for the advice Eddie," I choked out and fled.

Di I felt like he'd literally knocked the breath from me. How dare Eddie talk to me like that. I was shaking like pine colada mix in a blender. I composed myself as best I could and hurried down the hall to the ladies room. Through my haze of tears I spied Curtis and Debra walking towards me. I said good morning and rushed into the ladies room. I cried then washed my eyes and went back to my desk. Luckily I had plenty of work to keep me busy.

Lunchtime was a quiet. Curtis was perceptive enough to realize something was amiss. After asking me a couple of time if anything was wrong, he gave up and didn't push for an answer. I wasn't up to discussing my conversation with Eddie. Curtis adjusted his seat and took a nap. I read and that was that.

I didn't feel like meeting Curtis after work. So I rushed home and made a beeline for the mailbox. My funds were low and the child support check was due three days ago. I called Gerry Sr. and left a message on his answering machine explaining the situation.

The boys hadn't made it home yet. It was blessed quietness for a little while. Curtis hadn't mentioned the state of affairs with Retha today. That gave me pause. Before I knew it bedtime was upon me. I was more than ready for this day to be over. Eddie's words haunted me even as I fell asleep.

The blues got me locked up in chains
There will be no winning, no happiness and no gain
That man he just don't want to be mine
Peace of mind it eludes me, I can't seem to find

May 12

Today was a nice sunny day. The warm rays and the bright sky always put me in a good mood. Di do you want to take bets on how long that will last? I had a few voice mails that required my immediate attention when I arrived at work. One in particular was from Rick the third shift operations manager. I returned his call. We ended the conversation with I'd come and see him in an hour.

Thank God the company didn't call me early in the wee hours of the morning. Di I am on call 24/7, 365 days a year. So I must be available to my job, any time of the day or night, holidays don't even matter. I don't have a backup per se.

There have been times I've been on vacation and have still been gotten called or paged.

A while back, late one night I began experiencing stomach pains. As the hours progressed the pains became more severe. I went to acute care early the next morning. My doctor's office hadn't opened and I felt like I was dying.

The curtains parted, a doctor stepped into the cubicle and asked for my primary care physician's telephone number. I began to panic and thought there must be something horribly wrong. The doctor still hadn't given me any medication for the pain. I was moaning and groaning, scared and feeling alone. As I lay on the bed, dire thoughts raced through my head. When the doctor returned to the cubicle he informed me that he'd talked to my doctor. They concurred it was best I go to the hospital by ambulance.

Since my family resides in the city there was no one to call. I felt like a motherless child and was scared to death. The initial diagnosis was gallstones. As it turned out I had a bladder infection. I was given a prescription for antibiotics and advised to stay home the next five days.

Mykal picked me up from the hospital after I was released that evening. He was very concerned. Worry lines furrowed his brow.

After I returned home, I called my manager Mark and relayed the diagnosis and cure. He told me to take care of myself and stay in touch. Curtis came by the next day with flowers (at lunchtime of course). Two days later Mark telephoned. He frantically explained an emergency had arisen. Mark needed me to come into the office ASAP.

The medication had just started to kick in and I was feeling a little better. I told Mark that I'd be there when my son arrived home from school. Mykal drove me to my job fussing the entire time. Didn't the doctor tell me to stay in bed until next week? His voice seemed to drone on and on during the ride.

I got out of the car slowly. A couple of my co-workers were standing outside the entrance. They watched as I made my way slowly towards them. Then they began complaining. Mark could have sent the work home to me instead of me coming in. The bottom line was the work just should have waited until I was able to come back to work. I collected the assignment and crept slower back to the car. I dozed off as Mykal drove home.

When I arrived home, I felt as bad as I had the day I went to the hospital. Needless to say, I completed the task and was named Employee of the Month of my team. Sorry Di I digress yet again.

My place of employment is a one story red brick building. Glass covers the entire length of it. I glanced outside as I walked down to Rick's office. Whom do I see but Curtis with Debra with by his side. She stood close like she was stuck to him with glue. I made a mental note to ask Curtis what was up with that? One second thought, I'll stop by his office when I finish talking to Rick.

Thirty minutes later Rick and I were done. I almost hate attending meetings or discussing issues with my co-workers. It usually equates to more work for me.

I headed to Curtis' office. As I got closer gales of laughter emanated from the room. Debra beat me to the punch. *Every time I turn around she's here.* I stepped inside Curtis' office and all laughter ceased.

Debra gave me a cool smile, "Good morning Marissa." She bid a hasty retreat. "Curtis I'll talk to you later," she added as she smiled secretively at him. "Where have you been?" Curtis asked moving papers on his desk.

I sat and explained, "I just finished meeting with Rick about a problem last night. So what's up with that?"

"Nothing to worry your pretty head about," he countered quickly. "How about meeting at the forest preserve for lunch? Let's stop at the deli for hot dogs?"

"I'll check my schedule and let you know," I replied haughtily as I left his office.

Well Di good moods don't last long at all sometimes. I made it back to my office my dignity intact. I put my phone on voice mail and once again dug into work. Gerry left a message in agreement with that I should have received the check by now. He said he'd make some calls and get back to me back later. Later to Gerry unfortunately could be days. He feels no sense of urgency about anything.

I was still a little steamed over Debra being over Curtis like a cheap suit. It seems lately every time I turn around she's always there. Her behavior wounds me deeply because I couldn't do the same.

According to Curtis it's not professional and he doesn't want the office in our business. I keep telling him they know about us anyway. We leave for lunch in separate cars and seldom return at the same time. The

85

only time we go to lunch in the same vehicle is to celebrate our birthdays. Or when we go to the hobby shop together. Then we travel in my car. No pda (public displays of affection) at least not near the job.

I know if I talked to any of my girlfriends about my love life they'd say he's playing me. Those sistahs would be on my case like white on rice.

I decided to have lunch alone and sent Curtis an email canceling our plans. I stopped at McDonald's and bought myself a sandwich then parked in the Forest preserves. I tried having a heart-to-heart talk with myself. I had to be honest if he cheats on Retha, then he damn well could be cheating on me with Debra. I want to win though...I want the prize and I just love the man.

We mustn't sit together, side by side
My emotions I keep closed and hide
Dropping me off at the door just won't do
Can't give away any hints of what's happening between meand you

May 13

Di Curtis called last night and jokingly asked me, "Is it that time of the month? Why are you so grumpy"

We talked then off to dream land for me. Today was quiet. No drama. No Debra. Curtis called tonight so not a bad day. I managed to be a good girl and didn't mention Retha once. Gerry as I'd known never called back.

Di I wonder if Adele and Corrine suspect Curtis lives with someone or assumes he's married. They've been calling more than usual lately. I don't know if they are happy in their marriages and if life is treating them well. They both attended the same college.

They did everything in a politically correct manner. By that I mean completed college, married and had children. They eventually went back to college and received their master degrees.

Adele works in the education field and Corrine the health care industry. Neither couple has any financial problems that I am aware of. They have mortgages on homes and the mandatory two cars per family. They both have the requisite 2.5 children.

Neither one has any vices like drinking or smoking. To me they are perfect women with perfect lives. I can't say I envy them. I am more comfortable with people with some type of vice or shortcoming. I don't mean drink like a fish or do drugs to the point where they consume your entire life just something.

Perfect people tend to just make me uneasy. It seems like it's a more level playing field when people are aware of each other's strengths and weaknesses. Deanna and I on the other hand do not fit that perfect mold. I wonder if it is because we aren't Momma's biological children?

May 14

In case I forgot to mention Curtis and I have several places we meet for our trysts. One is up the street near the expressway our after-work hangout. We frequent several spots in the forest preserves our favorite being the one with a duck pond. Since I get off work earlier than he does I usually wait for him there.

Today I parked in our usual spot. I happen to glance up and see a little black Toyota drive pass by. Complete a u-turn and then exit the parking lot. My mouth fell open it was Debra. Now what the hell is she doing here? Now Di I have to admit all of this had me shaken. It may be time for me to take my head out of the books and pay more attention to reality. Apparently something was up and by keeping my head in the books I'd almost missed it.

Curtis drove up twenty minutes later and joined me in my car. He leaned over and kissed me. I was fuming. "Guess who just drove by here?" I asked him. "Your first two choices don't count."

"Now what's wrong?" He asked impatiently.

"Well," I said slowly, "I am trying to figure out why Debra would drive to this particular spot. Then turn around and then leave? Do you have any ideas?"

He looked into my eyes and replied, "No. I don't. Not a clue."

I retorted heatedly, "You're lying."

We exchanged more words and left shortly. Parting had become such sorrow. Not sweet either. Di, he didn't call meand I certainly didn't page him.

Honesty is the best policy most people say
Unfortunately it doesn't seem very much to come my way
It appears telling the truth, it's elusive for you
You continue to lie or omit things, that's what you do

May 15

I woke up feeling depressed. It seems no matter how hard I try I can't win. But you know what flashed through my mind? What the hell am I going through this drama for? I can sense Curtis is lying to me. I can just feel it. My stomach rolled. I think I'll call in sick today. A mental health day is called for.

I logged onto the system left Mark an email and voice mail for good measure. I burrowed under the comforter. Sleep claimed me shortly. A rat-a-tat sounded at the door.

"Are you sick? Mom what's wrong?" Gerry Jr. asked?

I answered, "Nothing's wrong with me physically. I'm just a little tired."

"Are you going to work today?" Mykal inquired solicitously.

"No." I yawned. "I'm staying home."

I attempted my journey to dreamland again. The telephone rang. *Damn can't a Sistah get some sleep around here?* I leaned over and peered at the caller id unit.

It was Curtis concern in his voice, "Are you okay?"

I told him, "I'm fine. I just needed a time-out."

We decided to meet for lunch. I asked him to come out my way. "My house is empty lunch is on me." I meant that literally."

Curtis declined with a touch of remorse in his tone. "I'd never make it back to the office."

I turned over in the bed snuggled under the comforter and tried to go back to sleep. I rose later found something to eat and called Curtis. I told him where to meet me and volunteered to pick up lunch.

When I arrived he was parked and waiting.

After we finished eating Curtis remarked he was ready to meet my Momma. What did I think about going to see her after work next week?

I told him gleefully, "It's a plan." Then all too soon I was back home. The day blossomed into a good one. My check finally came. It was waiting in the mailbox. So I decided to treat the boys to dinner. We arrived home an hour and a half later.

The snoop sisters (Adele and Corrine) as I'd dubbed them called in their quest to get the 411 on Curtis. I knew where this conversation was headed. I could sense they were about to go into I want to get in your business mode.

Corrine didn't even bother to fake her curiosity. After asking how my family was doing, she asked if Curtis and his children were attending the barbeque. Corrine explained she was making a list of the attendees to arrive at a headcount.

I informed her that I wasn't sure yet. I'd let her know later in the week. Before they could bombard me with further questions, Gerry Jr. walked into the room yelling. He needed a ride for a game at school

The game was already underway so he wanted to leave ASAP. Thank God for children sometimes they come in handy. I bid my sisters a fond adieu after I told them I'd holler at them later.

May 16

It's Saturday and I'm spending the night at Holiday Inn out in Curtis' neck-of-the-woods. I do so every couple of months when it's Gerry's weekend with the boys. Curtis and I both live in the suburbs of Chicago, I reside in Aurora and he's in Park Forest. So we don't live remotely close to one another.

We have breakfast and lunch together and meet for a little while after work. But that's about it. He comes to my house from time to time. His excuse back in the day was that he didn't want to cause problems for me until my divorce was final. Unfortunately the practice continued long after the judge dissolved the marriage.

His theory was until he and Retha no longer share the same household that he had to honor and respect the relationship.

The downside to being involved with my down low lover is lack of time specifically quality time. We've never spent one night together except for business trips. I can't ever call him. The biggest farce of all is no one at work is supposed to know about our relationship. In reality I'm sure we're the targets of gossip big time.

In fact this past Christmas my Director hosted a party. He made a point of telling me Curtis was invited also.

Let me state my case. Retha was scheduled for an overnight business trip. Curtis and I made plans. His kids were going to spend the night with his brother. I talked Gerry into keeping the boys overnight.

We planned a romantic candlelight dinner and even toyed with the idea of taking off the next day. Retha wasn't due to return until late the following evening.

She cut the trip short and came back the same day. He even had to leave work early to pick her up at the airport. So I come out his way ever so often.

The jarring ring of the telephone awakened me. "I'm on my way," Curtis whispered sexily into the telephone.

That was all I needed to hear. Shivers ran up and down my spine. Twenty minutes later a knock sounded at the door. The waiting was finally over. Curtis stopped at a restaurant and picked up breakfast. "How soon do you have to be back?" I asked as we ate.

He answered as he rubbed his hands together, "I think I can fit you in for an hour or two. Then I'll head back home and see you later on today. She's scheduled appointments to look at apartments today and tomorrow."

Well Di nature took its course and we got busy and you know how I love to get busy with my dll. Curtis left

93

about an hour and a half later. He showered, dressed, and told me to be ready for round two later. I was awash in the afterglow of love. I'm sure I was purring like a cat who just finished lapping a bowl of cream.

Di my favorite hobby is reading first and foremost. I love doing challenging crossword puzzles. Music and watching sports, basketball and football are some of my other pastimes.

Curtis and I participate in the football pool and purchase squares. Guess which one of us was the cause of us losing last season? Hint not me.

Many Sunday afternoons he'll call to ask if I'd seen a particular play. I can definitely keep myself entertained. I snuggled under the covers. Curtis called me around seven o'clock that evening. It was time for round two. Let the games begin.

A liquid fire burns between the two of us
That thin line between love and lust
Starting with a simple kiss from you
Traveling through my body I don't know what to do

May 17

Di there was a soft rap the door around eight thirty this morning. When I opened the door Curtis stood smiling before me. He clutched a bag of bagels in one hand. Retha had gone to look at more apartments. Charles and Curtis stayed were out having breakfast with Curtis's brother 's family. We made up for more lost time after eating and then chilled.

We decided to see a movie. A simple activity we'd never shared before. We headed towards our cars.

Curtis made a quick detour, walked to my car and proceeded to talk me into going to his house. Di I was adamantly against the idea. He pleaded with me, "I've been to your house many times. It's time for you to see mine."

After much cajoling on his part I conceded. A short time later we arrived at his place of residence. Curtis hopped out of his car. During the drive I became nervous not to mention a little paranoid. What if Retha comes back? The Avon Lady no longer comes calling door to door. Maybe I could pretend to be a Jehovah Witness.

I worked myself into a tizzy. As I exited the car my legs felt limp as overcooked spaghetti. I was shaking like a leaf blowing in the wind. My distaste for the whole idea must have shown on my face.

Curtis looked at me asked, "What's wrong?"

I told him, "I'm not feeling this. Not at all." I shakily made my way over the threshold.

Then curiosity got the best of me. The house was nicely decorated. For a place Curtis claimed the lady of the house didn't pull her cleaning share, the house was immaculate. I remarked as much to Curtis. He reminded me that he cleans every Saturday morning.

Curtis gave me on a tour of the house. We spent extra time in the basement his domain Curtis' model trains and planes are displayed. Many a lunch break we'd go to the hobby shop and pick up supplies. I felt like some of them belonged to me since I'd picked out some of the models.

Hell Di I've even constructed some of them myself. I admit I'm not mechanically inclined. Curtis usually has to rebuild them after I'm done. He gives me an A for effort though. I do a better job of painting the accessories than anything else. His hobby is important to him so I try to share it with him.

The tour ended upstairs where the bedrooms were located. Christine's was very girlish painted pink with white borders. Posters of her favorite musical artist decorated the walls.

Charles' was a typical teenage boy's room messy. Basketball and football players were his choice of posters.

At last we stood at the doorway of the master bedroom. It was tastefully designed but a little too masculine for my taste. My eyes became glued to the bed. The bed Curtis and Retha share. A big king sized black lacquered one.

I have no business in this room scurried across my mind. Curtis insists they don't make love much. When I come out his way he says he saves himself for me. (Yeah right). Reality set in for me at that moment. Curtis, Retha and the kids are truly a family of sorts. What in the hell was I doing?

I stumbled a bit as I backed out of the room and down the stairs. Curtis still didn't have a clue of the emotions raging through me like a brush fire in a forest.

I sighed and told him, "I'm ready to go."

He replied, "We still have time. Can I get you something to eat or drink?"

I said more forcefully, "I'm just ready to go. Can we leave now?"

Fifteen minutes later we pulled back into the hotel parking lot. I checked out. We went to the movie theater and enjoyed an action movie. I passed on lunch and took my behind back to my part of town.

I was in a quiet mood when the boys returned home. They tried unsuccessfully to tease me out of my mood. It didn't work. Finally, they gave up after Mykal asked if it was that time of the month? I snapped.

Di, Curtis, Retha, Christine and Charles are really a family regardless what Curtis says. I don't know....

Yes another sleeps besides you at night
You turn to her for loving and it doesn't seem right
No you belong to another, someone else's man
I have to remember that I can I must I will I can

May 18

Di I felt refreshed after my weekend rendezvous. It was like I was floating on air. I swear my feet never touched the ground. Weekends away from home are equivalent to a time-out for me. I get a chance to escape reality the rat race and day-to-day routine of my life.

There was no Debra skulking in the background today. My world was *all good* on this morning. When Curtis and I had lunch, we reminisced about the first time he put the moves on me. Let me clarify that I should say when I finally took his intentions serious.

Gerry had moved to an apartment and we were waiting for the divorce to be granted. At the time I was talking to an old flame of sorts. Sorry Di there's no dirt for me to share with you. Corey and I only talked on the telephone. When my sisters and I were growing up we spent summers with my Grandmother in Mississippi. Auntee, Momma's older sister lived with Granny.

98

My aunt has twin nieces (They were my idols when I was a child) and a nephew (their brother) on her husband's side of the family. Corey is his name. We had crushes on each other as children. He'd teased me, show off and pull my hair. Those things little boys do when they're trying to get a little girl's attention. We lost contact with each other as we became older. I worked summer jobs when I turned fifteen year's old. Those times down home as Momma called them became a thing of the past.

One of the deaths that caused the radical change on my outlook of life was Auntee's, the aunt Corey and I shared. Momma, Gerry Jr. and myself traveled on the City of New Orleans train from Union Station in Chicago to Jackson Mississippi to handle Auntee's business.

Corey just happened to be visiting his mother at the time. As we talked Di something strange began happening to me. We conversed for hours (it seemed) standing in Auntee's front yard. He complimented me on my appearance and made me feel like desirable again. I hadn't experienced those types of feelings in a long time.

Later I realized just how much I missed attention from the opposite sex. He didn't say anything overt there was something about his body language. I noticed him giving me the once-over. I mentioned how I gained weigh over the years. He told me not to worry that I looked good!

We talked about our careers, marital status, (he was separated), sports and life in general. He invited me to his Mom's house to watch (you guessed Di,) a basketball game. I declined feeling frightened and just froze. I knew something unusual had happened to me.

The deep freeze I'd immersed myself in began to thaw. Unfortunately he lives in Texas. We exchanged telephone numbers. For a couple of months we talked on the phone once or twice a week. He was the male equivalent of my support system as I waited for my divorce to become final. Corey undertook the role willingly. After the divorce was a finalized we still talked but decided the long distance thing wouldn't work.

Back at the work place the office was ablaze with the news of my impending divorce. I'd been working there about seven years. No one had heard any hint of trouble regarding my marriage.

Curtis came by my office after he heard the news. First he said it took me long enough to make that move. How he'd been waiting a long time for me to become free.

Then his manners kicked in and he remembered most divorces are sad occasions and offered his condolences. He added if there was anything I needed, anything at all just say the word. He'd be there for me.

Quite a few men at the work place told me the same thing. Di it was like going from a wallflower to the belle of the ball. I guess divorce does that for you. It didn't hurt that I had also lost about ten pounds so I looked fantastic if I may say so myself.

My old managers Nelson remarked had he been ten years younger that he would have put himself in the running. He also asked me why women tended to look so much better after divorces? Why not during the marriage?

I told him it was all about motivation.

Anyway let me continue. Two members of the network team were scheduled to go to Washington D.C. for a seminar along with Curtis. Due to company politics I'd recently been reassigned to the network group.

My new manager Tom stopped by to see me that morning. He informed me one of the guys scheduled for the trip wouldn't be able to attend due to a death in the family. If I couldn't find a replacement within the next six hours, I would be required to take his place.

I was furious Di how could Tom inform me on such short notice that I had to go out of town? I have children to contend with teenage boys at that. I was in a foul mood the entire morning. Someone must have told Curtis about the change in plans. He came to my office and told me he was glad to hear I was going on the trip.

Curtis made the mistake of counting his chickens before they were hatched. He rented a car and said he could hardly wait for our weekend together. Did I think I could stay an extra night?

I was simultaneously s thrilled and offended. I felt his actions were too aggressive. After he left my office I picked up the telephone and began searching furiously for a replacement. By early afternoon I'd found my prey. A third shift operator committed after promising me effusively, he wouldn't let me down. I breathed a sigh of relief after I got off the telephone. I walked to Tom's office and sedately informed him that I wouldn't be going to the seminar.

After lunch I walked to the canteen to purchase a can of pepsi cola. Suddenly an angry voice roared behind me. Curtis stood behind me scowling furiously.

His voice raged with anger. How could I do that to him? The trip was the perfect opportunity for us to get to know each other better.

Curtis made plans. He rented a convertible to tour the city. Now I'd gone faked him out. What happened? Why wasn't I going?

Problem was Gerry and I were still married and I have a problem with committing adultery. Plus Di I was really taken aback at how high-handed Curtis acted. I'd never committed to the trip. He didn't have it like that not yet anyway. Brotha assumed too much and I informed him of that. I sure did right there in the canteen. My friend Liz witnessed his tirade.

As Curtis walked out of the area, she looked at me and broke into laughter. Liz smirked, "he's got a case for you girlfriend."

Upon hearing her remarks Curtis stomped louder and faster as he made a not so graceful exit. Liz and I cracked up. I laughed until tears streamed out of my eyes.

I still tease Curtis about that comedy as I call it every now and then. He says to this day that he doesn't find the situation funny. And complains about getting stuck with a white boy instead of me. It was not quite what he'd envisioned. We've definitely had good times. You'll hear. Later Di....

May 19

I broke a cardinal rule today and went to see Curtis twice in one day. That's a no- no. I'm allowed one visit per day. It dawned on me he hadn't mentioned Retha's situation lately. So I sashayed down the hallway and around the corner to his office.

"Curtis," I began seriously, "What's happening with Retha, did she find an apartment yet?"

Oh the plans we made when she finally leaves his house. I'd finally spend the night at his place. For sure the first weekend the boys were scheduled to stay with Gerry. Who knows maybe even the night same night. That's providing we could find places for the kids to

103

stay. He has a fireplace in his house Di. My weakness is fireplaces. I've never lived in a house that had one. His is adorned with a bearskin rug placed directly in front of it. We planned to wear the skin off that bear.

He answered hesitantly, "Nothing yet. She's still looking."

"What's the holdup?" I asked sitting on the edge of the seat.

"Nothing in particular. She just hasn't found anyplace to her liking yet."

"Okay," I sighed. "Are we on for lunch at 1130?"

"Sure baby." He smiled.

I went back to my office my mind wondering. I knew Curtis and I were at a crossroad. I didn't think it would take her this long to find housing. I felt if I backed down there would always be three of us (at this point maybe four) in this relationship.

I didn't get divorced to be involved in a love triangle. So I am going to have to stand firm for my own peace of mind. Curtis loves me I believe that and I love him. Time is dwindling. We're down to eleven days.

I worked diligently the rest of the morning and before long I was caught up on my projects.

That can however change at a moment's notice. My mind drifted to our first Christmas together. We didn't actually spend the day together but had a blast anyway. One Christmas Eve Curtis informed Retha he needed to finish shopping. He would be out of the house most of the day. We met at a mall and had breakfast. After the meal we hit the stores and shopped. Curtis and I actually shared eight uninterrupted hours without a telephone call from you know whom.

He bought sports jerseys for my boys. Mykals received the Green Bay Packer quarterback, Brett Farve. Gerry Jr. got the New York Knicks shooting guard John Starks. We went to the hobby shop where I purchased trains kits for Curtis.

I bought Charles Chicago Bears paraphernalia, a cap, sweatshirt, and gloves. Curtis wasn't quite ready for Christine to have a cell phone yet. I broke him down on as I gave him the pros and cons. He finally he gave in.

We stopped at a jewelry store and he asked if I saw anything I wanted. I advised him to surprise me. We looked at rings and a couple of wedding sets caught my eye.

Di my ex-husband Gerry could never get it right. I am a Christmas person and I'll spend the bucks to ensure everyone receives some of things on their lists. Money is no object. On Christmas day you'd see all three of my guys with stacks of gifts. I'd be lucky if I received three. To this day I can't figure out why. Gerry was just that type of guy at least with me. Most of the time I'd just give him a list with four or five items on it.

When Mykal received his paycheck from his first job the check was all of maybe forty dollars. He spent twenty of his hard earned earning on a NBA cap for me. I was touched but admonished him never to spend the majority of his check on me again.

My oldest son's explanation for actions was that on Christmas he, Gerry Jr. and their Dad always received so many gifts. I never got nearly as many presents. I related that story to Curtis. So I guess my dll was going to make up for all past Christmases.

Curtis pulled his car in my driveway. I stood at the window eagerly anticipating his arrival. He unloaded the trunk of his car and removed what seemed to be tons of presents. His gifts to the boys scored a big hit. They loved them.

Finally it was my turn. Di I swear I cried. He'd gotten me a leather jacket, a couple of books by my favorite authors, two Body and Soul CDs and an elegant gold lighter with both our names engraved on it. He also went to Victoria Secrets. I don't think I've ever received so many gifts in my entire life at one time. I felt overwhelmed.

Curtis' cell phone rang it was Christine. I'd sent his children's gifts home with him on Christmas Eve. She thanked me effusively for the cell phone and told me she loved me.

Our children are acquainted with each other (more on that later). The boys left the room to give us a little privacy. I hugged Curtis holding onto him as if for dear life. I thanked him by showering wet, juicy, kisses upon his cheeks and lips.

He simply said, "the best for the best. This is only the beginning. Stick around there's more in store for you."

Di in my heart I know this man cares for me. He just has too...

I find myself singing, smiling and humming
When I know you're on your way to me, just coming
That private special loving look you give to me
Love, come on I'm ready let us be

May 20

Di, today is M-day. Curtis is finally going to meet my Momma. I am excited and simultaneously scared. This visit was for him to meet Momma only. The sisters would receive their intro at a later date. Curtis and Momma have talked by telephone before. He called and wished her Happy Birthday earlier this year.

We'd planned to leave after work. I guess I should have been thankful for a little downtime yesterday. Today I was inundated with more projects. Curtis planned to leave work a half an hour early so we could bypass rush hour traffic.

We met at our usual place and Curtis immediately tried to back out of going. His excuses were Retha was becoming suspicious and he'd really like to do it another day. I informed him in no uncertain terms it was now or never. If he didn't accompany me our relationship was over. I was quaking with anger but didn't back down.

We glared at each other. My cell phone went off it was Momma. She was calling to verify that we were still coming and to let us know she'd prepared dinner. I looked Curtis dead in the eyes and said we were on the way.

When Curtis is upset he miraculously turns into a NASCAR driver. I was as mad as a wet hen as I followed him. We broke all kinds of speeding laws. When we reached the city limits I took the lead and he followed me to the house I grew up in.

Momma was waiting for us when we walked up the stairs. She hugged him. Then we sat in the dining room and chatted. Dinner was great and Curtis complimented her on her cooking. She positively beamed. I could sense her observing our interaction.

His cell phone rang and he went into the den to take the call. Momma shot me a look as if to say she liked what she saw. He had her stamp of approval.

We left to go home a couple of hours later. As we stood on the porch, Momma said something to him about treating her baby right.

Curtis replied, "No problem she's my baby too."

He promised he would come and see her again. He walked me to my car. Kissed me and said he'd call later to make sure I made it home okay.

Di to this day I don't know how I made it home in one piece. I should have been ecstatic since Curtis had finally met Momma. If he were playing me then he would not have made the effort.

Unfortunately I had to give him an ultimatum to do so. He said all the right things to her. But why did I have to force him to go with me kept crossing my mind. Finally I pulled the car into my driveway. The boys met me at the door and plied me with fifty questions.

"Did you and Curtis go to Grandmomma's house?" Mykal asked.

I nodded my head yes.

Gerry Jr. asked, "Did she cook and send anything for us?'

I told him to go out to the car their food was on the back seat. They know Martha Bailey. You never leave her house without taking something home with you usually food. I sat with them while they ate. Later, they went to their rooms to complete homework. I walked to my bedroom sat on the bed and sobbed.

My worst fears were coming true. Retha hadn't found an apartment and Debra was all over him. Let's not forget I'd literally had to force him to meet Momma. What else could go wrong today?

The telephone rang later that night. Mykal picked it up. I glanced down at caller id. It was Curtis. He and Mykal talked for a while. Then my son yelled, "Mom pick up. It's for you."

I put the receiver to my ear and sighed, "Hello."

Curtis said, "Hi. I just wanted to make sure you made it home all right."

I replied, "Yes I did. I'm getting ready for bed." How did you like Momma?"

"She was okay." He replied. "What do you think she thought of me?"

I answered, "I don't know?" We haven't talked about you yet. When I do I'd let you know."

After talking about nothing in particular we ended the call without saying our usual 'I love you'. Things seemed to be changing rapidly.

I got the blues so damn bad it hurts
I can't seem to make it right though I work and work
Still nothing remains except heartache and pain
Tears flowing down my face, burning like acid rain

May 21

Di after I awakening this morning, I sat on the side of the bed for a while. I lit a cigarette and decided I was not ready to face the world. I thought maybe today would be a good day to work from home.

I sat for a long time lost in thought and then stood up and walked into the bathroom. I looked in the mirror and didn't like what I saw. My eyes were puffy, swollen with sorrow. I opted to stay home. My telephone line would be tied up and I wouldn't have to worry about calls from anyone.

I pulled on my robe and headed to the basement powered up my pc and logged on. Not long after I started, Mark emailed me and asked me to reschedule a meeting. I replied with open dates and times.

Curtis meeting Momma yesterday brought reminded me of when I met Christine. She's a Daddy's girl and I knew I'd have acceptance issues with her. Curtis has often said his children sense he's not happy with his and Retha's relationship. They've asked many times why doesn't he just put her out. I'm with them on that. I like to know the answer to that question myself. Curtis said when Christine was a younger, she'd cry about not having a Mama like the other girls. He was hopeless when it came to combing her hair or picking out little girl's clothes. He was not into girlish activities. Part of his and Retha's agreement was she help him raise Christine.

Last year the Friday after Thanksgiving Curtis brought Christine to work with him. He asked me to meet him in the canteen. When I arrived she sat at our table with a sullen look on her face. I stared at her open-mouthed with amazement. She was a female version of Curtis. Christine is a very beautiful girl. I couldn't stop staring at her.

Her expression said loud and clear that she didn't want very much to do with me. I got the message. Curtis left the two of us alone and returned to his office. Talking to her was awkward for a while. I bravely forged ahead in my attempt to make conversation. Christine eventually thawed a smidgen.

We chatted about school. Curtis enrolled her in an all-girl Catholic prep high school. She wasn't happy there and subsequently her grades slipped after being a straight A student. Christine and Curtis bickered constantly. He initially planned for the three of us to have lunch together. Di I didn't want to come off pushy so I declined the invitation. Curtis was scheduled to work a half-day.

After I arrived home I thought about Curtis, Christine, Charles, my boys, and me. I feared Curtis and I weren't setting a good example for the children. We were sneaking around using the children as an excuse to see each other on the weekends.

Since then I'd won his children over and he in turn mine. Charles and Christine have visited my house and the kids seemed to get along fine. Curtis and I have looked at houses near the job. We knew we'd need a large one with our brood.

That's one of the reasons I thought Di that what we had was real. If he was just playing me why get the kids involved? And why bother to meet my Momma? If I'm honest with myself Curtis wasn't in any great hurry to meet Momma or my extended family.

The children are another story altogether. Curtis says he and Retha don't spend holidays together. He visits and dines with his family and she with hers. Another reason, I have hope our time is coming. He says they are not a *REAL* family. He says what he and Retha share is a pseudo family. So I have hopes Di big ones that the six of us would become a real family soon. Step one get Retha out of the picture.

Back to the present. I was done with work and off the system by two o'clock. As soon as I powered my pc down, the telephone rang. It was Curtis and he was furious with me. "You could have called me Rissa," he said angrily.

"Curtis," I said sweetly, "I meant to but got caught up with work." You know how it is sometimes."

"Let me guess," he added, "You're still upset about what happened yesterday?"

"No I am not mad or upset. Maybe disappointed would be a better description. I can't believe you didn't want to go see Momma. Hell it was your idea not mine anyway."

"Hmm I guess you're right." He conceded. "I guess I was just nervous. I don't know."

"Maybe you're just not ready to let Retha go," I threw in. "Maybe our relationship is a mistake."

"Now Rissa," he said, "Calm down. Let's not be hasty."

"Has Retha found someplace to stay yet?" I asked serenely. Inside I was seething with anger.

"No," he responded slowly, "But she is still looking."

"The first of the month is right around the corner Curtis. If she is not out of your house by then, adios amigo."

"She'll be out," he said firmly. "Do you feel like coming my way?"

"No. I'm cooking dinner. You're welcome to join us. Otherwise I'll see you tomorrow."

He didn't come. Curtis called later to allay my fears. He admonished me to keep the faith. Everything will all work out in the end he promised.

May 22

Di my emotions are seesawing like the ride at the playground. Up and down, up and down. I can't help but have misgivings. My sixth sense is telling me I can't win.

Too bad it didn't tell me to not to get involved two years ago and I wouldn't be in the predicament today.

Debra wasn't hanging all over Curtis today. I attended her two o'clock meeting. I know I must have made her nervous because she kept mispronouncing and stumbling over her words.

If this whole situation wasn't so pathetic I'd feel sorry for her. You know what's funny before all this drama started with Curtis we used to talk. She's loves to read like I do and when we'd run into each other in the hallway, we'd talk about books we'd read. Then the big infatuation occurred and things haven't been the same since between.

Mykal has a baseball game tonight so I'll put in an appearance. I wouldn't mind attending more games but I'd have to contend with Gerry Sr.'s presence. Divorce to me means never having to see your ex unless you want to. That's my philosophy.

Today wasn't too bad. Curtis and I went to the hobby shop to look at a new model train set He's considering pre-ordering it. I love the hobby shop. The guys who work there think Curtis and I are married. They've called me his wife on more than one occasion and Curtis hasn't corrected them.

I paged him tonight and yes he returned the call.

Mykal's team won the game. He was in seventh heaven. I got lucky and Gerry Sr. didn't make it. An emergency arose at his job. The workweek is finally over and the onset of the dreaded three-day holiday weekend.

I didn't listen when my head said to leave you alone
I thought I can handle it be mature and fully-grown
I never thought a time would come when
We wouldn't be together
Not one entire day nor one night not now or ever

The boys reluctantly assisted with housecleaning this morning. They both swear they're never going to get married and plan on having maid service. So they don't have a reason to learn that kind of stuff. I've calmly told them about the best-laid plans not to mention Murphy's Law.

If remaining single was part of their future plans then they need to know how to cook and clean. So once a month we all pitch in and just get the dirty deeds done.

I prepared spaghetti and picked up a couple of cases of pop. The boys had no plans for the night. So we rented movies and stayed glued to the tube. They asked me if Curtis and company were coming tomorrow. No need getting their hopes up. I replied, "I doubt it."

Mykal gave me a funny look. Then all too soon we were in our respective bedrooms. The boys have their own rooms. Different rap songs blasted from both.

I yelled as always, "Turn it down."

The telephone rang. Curtis. Mykal picked up. Later Gerry Jr. conversed with him.

Finally it was my turn. I asked about his day. He said he stayed in the house all day and worked on his model trains. He slept and took it easy. He said his aunt Vicki was hosting the family barbeque, tomorrow as a matter of fact. He planned on going to the outing and maybe stop at Corrine's house.

Like a fool I got my hopes up. Maybe he'd show up this time. Come to think of it he didn't mention Retha and what happened with the apartment hunting. I paged him but didn't get a response.

Di I am so nervous. I can see it now. Curtis will probably come to Corrine's, and break the new to me gently. Something came up and Retha wouldn't be leaving after all. I know his moves.

Our relationship is a true testament to Maze's song, 'Joy and Pain.' It's always that joy and pain, sunshine and rain. It's never just one or the other for a little while. I guess I'll have to prepare for the worst. I know it's coming. I'll have to make a decision. I'll know by the first what I'm going to do.

We have our ups and downs good times and bad
We get on each other's nerves make each other made
But when I think of that precious smiling face
My heart starts to beat at a rapid pace

May 24

I was up bright and early as usual. The boys came
out of their bedrooms about noon. We had breakfast,
dressed, packed the car and headed to the city. The
travel time wasn't too bad. I pulled into Corrine's
driveway an hour later. We exchanged greetings with
everyone. The boys took the food and pop out of my car

Momma quizzed the boys about school. She also
asked about their plans for the summer. Did they have
girlfriends yet? Mykal stated he was a player. Gerry Jr.
said he had his eyes on a fine little honey. It was nice
seeing everyone. Sam's parents and brother along with
his wife and three children were in attendance as well.
The barbeque was scheduled to start at three o'clock.
When those two hose the barbeque dinner is always late.
By five we were digging in.

After we finished eating I tried paging Curtis but
didn't get a call back. He called me back around six-
thirty. "How are you doing? Have you eaten yet?" He
asked.

His family was still at his aunt's. I told him the day
had been predictable. We were late eating and everyone
wanted to know if he was making an appearance.

Curtis answered, "not this time."

I walked into the house. I knew this conversation was not going to be a pleasant one and I didn't want to give my sisters fuel for fire.

"Why can't you come? Just this one time?"

He went on to explain, because he's still living with Retha. He didn't think the timing was right to meet the rest of my family. He wanted things to be perfect when he met everyone.

"Just be patience." He scolded me.

I ended the call saying, "You go ahead and do what you have to do."

I was quite calm. In that place where I had almost let go and it didn't hurt as bad as it would. Not yet anyway. Curtis promised to visit me tomorrow. He swore that he wouldn't let me down. I told him I'd talk to him and just left it at that.

The rest of the evening passed by in a blur. I was in a reflective mood after our conversation. Mercifully no one asked if Curtis was coming to the barbeque. Finally it was time to go home or west young man, as I am fond of saying to Mykal. I tossed him the keys and told him he had the honor of driving home.

He grinned from ear to ear. My son has his own vehicle but loves driving my car. I have a Bonneville and it's my third baby. I'd bought him a car earlier this year.

Mykal and I went to a dealership located in a southern suburb. Curtis met us there and we left with a nice little car for Mykal. Before we parted ways we had lunch. Yes Di we've had some good times and know good things come to an end. I dozed off on the way home and then went to bed.

May 25

I made a grocery store run this morning and picked up ribs, chicken and ground beef. In case Curtis showed up. Today is actually the holiday. The boys will spend the day with Gerry and his family. I didn't want them to stay home waiting on Curtis knowing it was a good possibility they might not show.

I went into the kitchen and began preparing my side dishes more spaghetti and baked beans. I'd bought potato salad, (too much work) and made cole slaw. Gerry arrived at noon Gerry to collect the boys. I was on my own.

The day was nice and warm. Usually the weather is cool in Chi-town around Memorial Day weekend. I rummaged around the garage and found a couple of folding chair. I grabbed a wine cooler out of the fridge and sat outside reading, drinking, cooking my meat and listening to music.

The telephone rang about two o'clock. Curtis asked if the food was ready.

I replied, "There is food here with your name carved into it just waiting to be cooked."

Curtis laughed, "Give me half an hour. I'll see what I can do."

Charles and Christine were spending the day with friends. I must have dozed off. There was a feather light kiss on my neck. I jumped and Curtis stood over me. I greeted him with a big hug and kiss.

We went to the kitchen and returned with slabs of meat. A couple of hours later we were done cooking. Each of us showed off our culinary skills.

His cell phone went off a couple of times. He checked it and allowed it to go to voice mail. I knew the boys wouldn't return home until eight or nine o'clock that evening. So I pulled Curtis into my bedroom and showed my appreciation for his appearance.

Later we showered and went outside and pulled out a table out of the garage and dined outdoors.

Contentment showed on my sun kissed face. On the other hand I felt something was amiss. Was there a big kiss off in the cards for me? Was Retha really leaving? I had a lot on my mind. I didn't want to spoil the mood but I needed to know.

I decided to hold my piece. The first of the month is right around the corner. This could very well be the last time I spent with Curtis. I decided to just enjoy the moment.

The boys arrived home a little after eight o'clock. They don't enjoy spending time with Gerry's family as much as mine. They love their Grandma Patton's cooking. The boys feel they're blessed. They have two grandmothers who can throw down when it comes to cooking. So they were full and starting to get that droopy 'I ate too much look'. Gerry Jr. asked Curtis if Charles was coming over to spend a night soon.

Curtis winked at me and answered, "I think that can be arranged."

I gave the boys that okay already look and they bid Curtis goodnight. Di it was a good day one of joy and pain. Joy that he'd made the effort and finally spent a holiday with me. Pain that he didn't make it to Corrine's yesterday. Maybe that's what life is about and I just don't get it yet.

My joy and pain are one and the same
I saw, I loved, I ran, I came
I pray for strength to get through this
Mine and only mine, is my prayer and wish

May 26

Di spending time with my family recalled more painful memories. When Auntee passed Momma and I discovered she'd left a will. In retrospect Momma was probably aware of it all along. My aunt had a safe deposit box and Momma (surprise, surprise) had the key to it.

My aunt essentially left all her worldly possessions to her sister along with her nieces Adele and Corrine. Deanna and I weren't mentioned. I remember after reading it how devastated I felt. Momma could see I was upset but didn't say much. Out of respect for her grief I didn't mention my feelings either. Corrine always said we were a family that got along. No problems, issues or arguments the Perfect Family.

Perusing that document meant we non-biological daughters were not accepted by the extended family. Auntee was Momma's sister and she hadn't bothered to acknowledge either of Deana or me. It took all I had in me to maintain self-control. I felt as if someone had stabbed me in the heart.

I yearned to ask Momma how this turn of events transpired. Why were we left out of the will? Sometimes I think I was just too afraid to hear the answers.

We were brought up as *real sisters*. Momma would always tell people she treated all of us the same and made no differences. If that was the case, how did we come to this point in life? Especially with her sister

124

someone she was very close to. I held tightly onto my emotions. To this day I really don't know how I managed to so.

When I stepped into the shower that night my disappointment and frustrations erupted. As the streams of water hit my face the tears spilled. It felt like I'd cried for hours the water mixed with tears. I couldn't stop shaking. It was all I could do to keep from hollering aloud. When I came out of the shower, Momma was asleep.

My throat was raw. I could barely swallow. My eyes felt like tightly laced gym shoes. Tears kept leaking from my eyes like a drippy water faucet. I lost myself.

That's the only way I can describe my feelings. I was no longer the person I thought I was. One of my identities was Martha Bailey's daughter, Aunt Elizabeth and Auntee's niece. At that moment I didn't have a clue as to who I was anymore. It was one of most depressing times of my life.

No Di I've never confronted or talked to Momma about how I felt. What could she really say? I guess she was too wrapped up in her own sadness to notice mine. I'm not sure I talked to Gerry about what happened. More than likely I didn't. I remembered his response when I tried to talk to him about issues with my sisters and didn't even want to go there.

After that day it was like my definition of my place in the family was altered. Di I brooded over those events for a long time. I talked to Pam. She reiterated I'd have to confront them one day. She told me doing so might cause me pain. Don't do anything rash that I'd know when the time was right.

Later I remembered past incidents that I'd sort of glossed over. My family is somewhat judgmental and opinionated Di. My worst fear as a teenager was having to tell Momma that I was pregnant.

Thank God the situation never came to be. I think I would have committed suicide rather than tell her I was having a baby. I'd feel like I'd let her down.

To be honest Di I was judgmental and opinionated myself. All of that changed when I moved to the suburbs away from my family. Over the course of years I've met and talked to many people and I learned there is no such thing as a perfect family. Family is there for you, regardless of the problem. Family is also about accepting and loving all members of the clan as they are unconditionally.

The family Corrine described didn't exist. We gather together on holidays. And that's a good thing. Many families don't even do that. We never vacation together. In fact Di, Corrine and Sam own a time-share in Illinois. Adele and Corrine's families along with Momma go there every year.

I asked Adele last year to let Deanna and myself know what their plans were. Maybe we could all meet up for a day. You guessed Di nothing was ever said.

In effect my friends became my family. They supply emotional support when I need it. If anything is mentioned to Momma regarding problems and she doesn't agree with you then your issues become classified as mess. To be fair she'll listen to you and of course offer her opinion, the correct resolution in her mind. Things deteriorated to the point where I stopped talking about my problems. I didn't want to become the daughter or sister who started mess. You know what I mean deviate from the portrait of the perfect family.

D I hope when the boys make mistakes traveling along the road of life, I'll possess the same wisdom as my friends and listen... I felt I had to be perfect to be accepted by my family. Since I never knew of my sisters ever having problems I felt they were perfect. I'd call Adele and Corrine the perfect girls. I want my boys to live their life and not be afraid to make mistakes. Only through those mistakes do you learn about life, your strengths and weaknesses. Nobody is perfect.

As I said I'm a slow learner (smile) but I'm getting there. Boy did I let off some steam.

It hurt me so deeply cutting down to the core
You see I didn't know who I was anymore

The blinders have been torn away from my eyes
I could then see all the half-truths the stories and lies

May 27

Today at work today there wasn't as much pep in my step. I never know what's going to hit me. On the plus side my annual review is today so I have something to look forward to. Curtis and I met for breakfast. By ten o'clock I was in seated in Mark's office discussing my review. It went pretty much as I expected.

Di if I am not as successful in other aspects of my life I definitely excel at work. I've been called an over-achiever and anal-retentive. I don't mess around with the benjamins. I like my job the challenge and the work itself. I can do without the stress and lack of backup at times. They compensate me nicely though. I have been Employee of the Month at least twice a year since the award was implemented.

Last month Curtis and I won for our respective departments. We both go above and beyond duty when performing our jobs. My review was excellent. On the downside my pay increase was only five percent. Mark informed me that I'd be going to New Jersey for our disaster recovery test. I usually alternate with another team member.

Di I just have to tell you about the first time I went to Jersey. I went there maybe three months after my divorce. Curtis made plans like he did for the Washington trip. This time I was up for the challenge. He'd planned on renting a car and I told him that I wanted to visit the Big Apple. The group was staying at the Embassy Suites hotel. I was excited about the trip. We flew on the same Delta flight.

Curtis and I usually work the wee hours of the night during testing. We weren't scheduled to be at the site until midnight. We had the entire day or so I thought to spend together. On our agenda was a trip to New York. Imagine my surprise when I arrived in the lobby and another co-worker, a white woman Paula waiting also. She didn't want to go to New York so we drove through New Jersey instead. Newark wasn't my city of choice for touring.

Man, I thought, *what's happening here? Why is she here?* I was polite but irritated as hell. We had lunch and returned to the hotel. After parting ways we retired to our respective rooms to rest. I shook my head in disbelief as I lay on the bed. Remember I'm slow Di I didn't get it.

Later Curtis called and asked what I was I doing. Resting I informed him. He inquired about my dinner plans. I told him I'd planned on ordering room service.

"Do you want company?"

I half-heartedly told him said yes while visions of Paula danced in my head. I figured at that point it was too early in the relationship to make waves. We hung up.

After settling comfortably on a chair I asked Curtis what was up with Paula. I believe in asking what you want to know except when it comes to my perfect family.

He leaned forward on the bed and candidly explained Paula invited herself along. He couldn't get rid of her. Di, that alone should have been a sign of things to come. But I didn't know any better. He ordered room service and a movie.

Those few hours became our official first date. We talked and laughed at the movie. And got to know each other better. No, I didn't give him some at least not on that trip.

After dinner I returned to my room and prepared for the long night ahead. Curtis called to awaken me and instructed me to meet him the lobby.

Our work is intertwined to a large extent. I did my thing then he did his. If the day had progressed differently perhaps I would have sat with him. But I still felt a little put out from lunch.

Curtis sat on one side of the room and I on the other. We were within eyesight of each other though. He'd make funny faces at me from time to time. Or mouth kisses.

Before long my portion of the test was complete. My telecommunications lines were up and active. I noticed a good-looking young man who apparently worked for the disaster site giving me THE look. He was light brown skinned with a muscular built. I knew I couldn't flirt too tough with Curtis across the room.

Soon other technicians joined Curtis. He waved me over. In our field there are very few African-Americans especially women. So when we all meet up, male or female, there is usually camaraderie between us. Sometimes I think we're just glad to see another of our kind in the mix.

The guys mentioned had they known we were participating in the test they would have planned something for us to do.

I asked sweetly would New York have been on the itinerary?

The fine brother replied, "No doubt." He mentioned he was from the islands Jamaica. A Caribbean fest was scheduled the weekend in Queens. Today was the kick-off. He would have loved to show me the sights. His eyes traveled along my body.

I noticed Curtis was paying attention to our conversation. I bet there were other places this guy would have taken me floated across my mind. I think I would be correct in assuming I would have enjoyed myself. Best of all there wouldn't have been a third party involved.

After we shot the breeze for a while I returned to my seat.

Curtis came over and remarked he didn't bite. Why don't I sit a little closer?

Picking up my purse, bag and jacket, I moved to his side of the room. As time elapsed I needed to go to the bathroom. I have a horrendous sense of direction and got lost. I felt someone's warm breath tickling my neck. I just knew it was Curtis. Then a deep voice resounded in my ear asking if I was lost?

Di that deep baritone in my ear not to mention that accent caused me to nearly jump out of and wet my pants simultaneously.

Batting my eyes innocently I said I was lost.

He graciously offered to show me the way back to the test area. It was the fine brother and his name was Andre. We talked for a while. He told me I looked stunning and he'd like to get to know me better. He added he'd wished he'd known I was making the trip. Andre asked was if this my first trip to New Jersey? I smiled and told him no.

Before I knew what was happening he slid his business card into my front jean pocket and asked me how long I planned on being in the area.

Regretfully I told him we planned on departing the following day. Andre asked for my telephone number. I told him since I had his number that maybe just maybe, I'd give him a call. He escorted me back to the test area.

I'm sure guilt was written all over my face since Curtis asked what took so long. I told him that I'd taken a wrong turn.

He looked at me sharply then turned back to his terminal and resumed working. Later I discovered Paula was indeed trying to put the moves on Curtis. He eventually set her straight.

I got around to calling Andre. But alas his situation was worst than Curtis' he was married. I have a lot to consider. Maybe reading this journal will help me to stay focused on the task at hand. What do you think?

May 28

Reminiscing brought back memories of my business trip to Philly with Curtis and Eddie. Their mission was to install hardware at our Philadelphia office. Then we'd head to New Jersey for a two-day seminar. To learn to install and use new hardware the company recently purchased.

The trip lasted three days. I'd never been to New Jersey and was eager to visit Atlantic City. I planned to stroll the boardwalk.

At that time I was still married to Gerry. He and the boys drove me to the airport. I introduced everyone and killed time until it was time to board the plane. Curtis and Eddie slept. I read during the flight. We arrived in Pennsylvania in no time.

Eddie rented a car. Soon we arrived at our customer service offices. I talked with the employees while the guys did their thing. After they finished we went to lunch and were on our way to Vernon Hills, New Jersey.

We decided to stay in the hotel that night since we spent most of the day traveling. Class started at eight o'clock the following morning. Eddie asked if Chinese food was okay for dinner. I said sure. They departed and said they'd give me a jingle when they returned.

Thirty minutes later they returned. My stomach growled from the aromas emanating from the bags.

In a short time we demolished the feast. They'd also picked up beer and wine. We drank and sat around just shooting the breeze. Our conversation topics were current events, our kids, hopes and dreams and of course work. We decided to hit the casino after class.

Curtis knocked at my door the next morning. He decided to personally deliver my wake-up call. I told him I was flattered but his doing so wasn't necessary. I could sense mild flirting on his part. I caught him staring at me a couple of times during the ride yesterday. There was a blossoming attraction between us. But I was married. There was no getting around that fact. I hadn't met many men over the years that caught my attention. Curtis definitely did during the trip.

The focus of the class that morning was hardware. So there wasn't much for me to do. The agenda stated my portion would begin after lunch.

We hurried to the hotel showered, changed clothes and in no time were on our way to Atlantic City. I told the guys I didn't want to stay out late due to class the next morning.

The hotel was about sixty miles south of Atlantic City. Traffic was fairly light and we arrived in no time.

Our first stop was the Taj Mahal a Trump casino and hotel where we had dinner. We planned to hit the casino after the meal. The restaurant was elegant and dinner was appetizing.

I'd never been to a casino before so I was excited. Di as you can probably guess I don't get out much. The view of the Atlantic Ocean was enchanting. The waves billowed back and forth along the shoreline. I was simply enchanted. I wandered through the casino taking in the scenery. It was gaudy but emitted high excitement.

I went to the cashier and purchased fifty dollars worth of chips. It was time to see if lady luck was on my side. An hour later Curtis stood beside me and asked how it was going.

I said excitedly, "I'm winning!"

He replied flirtatiously, "I always knew you were a winner." His gaze was suggestive.

My stomach did a little flip-flop. I wondered if he would knock on my door tonight. Better still would I turn him away? I was definitely aware of him a quiescent male alpha animal.

Curtis put my arm in his and suggested we take a break.

We strolled along the boardwalk. As we walked a light misty rain began pouring. Don't ask me how Di but Curtis managed to produce an umbrella. In one fluid motion he put it up. Then put his arm lightly around my waist. We walked back inside the casino.

I continued playing the slots. Curtis returned later to inform me that he and Eddie would be at the blackjack table. Di I hit the jackpot a couple of times. The cocktail waitress brought a cup to put my winnings in. I kept playing and pretty soon my cup runneth over. I lost track of time.

Eddie and Curtis came looking for me around nine thirty. I was reluctant to leave just yet. Please I was still winning. They reminded me of class and how we still had long drive ahead of us. I begged for thirty more minutes, they acquiesced.

Forty-five minutes later I stood in front of the cashier cashing my chips. I had won maybe a couple of hundred dollars. I found the guys sitting in chairs at the lobby sleep written all over their faces.

"I won." I told them gleefully.

Curtis laughed, "It's about time. Let's go."

The men surmised I'd want to be in the bed by ten o'clock. They'd pegged as an early bird. They found out instead that I am capable of flipping the switch and becoming Ms. Night Owl when I so choose. I hadn't had so much fun in a long time.

I came to know Eddie and Curtis quite well during that trip. All pretensions were dropped. We talked openly and got to know each other.

Eddie was the only African-American in the Hardware Installation department, Curtis the only African American in Telecommunications and I am the only Black person in Technical Support. A friendship was born as a result of that trip.

After we returned to work, we made a promise to have lunch together quarterly. We dubbed ourselves you guessed 'The Onlies'. We pooled our money. I guess being the only female of the group, they asked me to hold the money.

Curtis later admitted he felt the same attraction and was sorely tempted. He said the only reason he didn't was because I was a nice person and married. He didn't want to cause problems or make waves.

Well we know what came of that don't we Di?

Your smile says to me, 'baby you're the best'
You're head and shoulders above the rest
It holds promise of good things to come
Excitement, joy, pleasure and fun

May 29

Di, I've definitely digressed quite a bit. Just bare with me the month is almost over. Today was quiet and uneventful. The boys are elated school will end in a week. They usually stay with Gerry the entire summer. He lives a couple of miles away from us. So they are in and out of the house all the time. Sometimes it feels like they never left.

Curtis hasn't mentioned Retha in a couple of days so I know what's coming. It's Friday and the weekend is almost upon us. I'm almost glad I won't see Curtis. I need time to decide my fate.

Back down memory lane again. About six months ago I was walking to the bathroom. I noticed Curtis leaving the building. I started to run outside and ask him what was wrong but didn't. When I returned to my desk he left me a voice mail saying he didn't feel well and was going home.

Curtis sounded horrible so I could tell something was terribly wrong. I paged him a few times but didn't get a return call. I was on pins and needles the whole time.

He finally called in the afternoon. He'd gone to the hospital and they'd admitted him and were running tests. I was beside myself with worry. A few hours later he called to inform me he was diagnosed with gallstones. The doctor was hoping the stones would pass during the night. If not Curtis would require surgery. I could tell he was out of it. I began sniffling.

Amused Curtis asked, "what's up with that? I'm the one sick. The pain was unlike anything I've experienced. I thought I was dying."

I asked, "What possessed you to drive home? You could have asked me to take you to the hospital or at the very least called Retha. "

"Come on now," he chuckled cynically.

"You come on now. After all it was an emergency."

When he called before he left work he'd planned to ask me to drive him to the hospital. As luck would have it I wasn't at my desk. Curtis managed to make it home and then call an ambulance.

I felt guilty here was opportunity to step up to the plate and I was probably running my mouth talking to Sharon. I made Curtis promise to keep me posted. I don't know how I made it through the rest of my workday Di but somehow I did. I rushed home, ran to my bedroom, closed the door and cried like a baby.

Mykal happened to come home. He heard me crying and asked what was wrong. I explained Curtis was sick and in the hospital.

He asked, "Why are you still at home? Do you need me to drive me to the hospital? "

I'd never told the boys Curtis was living with someone. I spilled the beans then.

Mykal peered at me with a puzzled look on his face and said, "wow Mom, this is blowing my mind. What do you want to do?"

I babbled sobbing, "I can't do anything except wait on Curtis to call me back."

He awkwardly patted my back trying to be comforting. Before I went to sleep Curtis called again. "I know you're upset because you haven't see me. Retha just left and why don't you come now?"

I lamented, "I can't. By the time I'd arrive at the hospital visiting hours will be over."

His response was to come anyway. He'd tell the nursing staff that I was his wife.

I asked subdued, "What if Retha comes back?" I declined the offer not wanting to take that chance.

Curtis called one more time around midnight and told me he me he loved me. How he was sure everything was going to be okay. He asked me to keep my fingers crossed for him that the stones would pass during the night.

I replied fervently, "You're always in my prayers. Don't worry about me, I'll be fine and we'll talk in the morning."

Di I just knew the Lord wouldn't take my soul mate from me not when I'd found him. The next morning almost as soon as I arrived at work Curtis called. The stones had indeed passed. He would be sent home tomorrow if all went well. He warned me not to even send flowers.

Curtis was released from the hospital the next day. The man was back at work within two days. I told him, he should stay home and rest. But he wasn't having it. He said he couldn't let any more days elapse without seeing my face. You know me, Di. I melted. Even when things were tough and he was out for the count my dll still came through for me. My first regret was not being there for him. My second was that I couldn't go to the hospital and see him for myself. That hurt Di it hurt bad.

It seemed after the gall stone incident as we called it, Curtis began to experience health problems. He was diagnosed with hypertension. We changed our eating habits and checked his pressure periodically during lunchtime. A couple of times it had risen dangerously high. I had to pressure him to call his doctor. It seemed we ate more Chinese food then I ever had in my entire life. I like it but not like that. He also became afflicted with gout. That was another scary moment.

Christine spent a night at my house. I have a niece Sherry the same age as Christine. She slept over also. When Curtis and Charles brought Christine to my house, I noticed he was limping. I asked worried, "What's wrong?

He complained, "My foot is killing me."

We retraced his activities and tried to determine if he'd injured himself in some way. I drew hot water and he soaked his foot. Unfortunately that didn't seem to help. He left a few hours later and said he'd pick up Christine tomorrow. The girls and I had a good time. We went out for lunch and then hit the mall. I treated them to a visit to a nail salon.

Curtis called a couple of times during the night. The girls went to a party with Mykal. He'd even allowed Gerry Jr. to tag along. I was on pins and needles the entire time they were gone. I told Mykal he'd better have the girls back on time. If he missed curfew then his butt was mine.

Monday was a holiday from school for the kids. Curtis called early the next morning to report he was still in acute pain. I called in sick and Di I broke another rule and drove out to his house. Retha was gone to work. When I pulled in front of his house, he hobbled out to the car.

I drove to the emergency room of the nearest hospital. That time the diagnosis was gout. It seemed we were at the hospital for years. Finally he was released. I stopped at a pharmacy to get his prescription filled. Then I dropped him off at home. I trekked back to my house since I'd have to take Christine home. During the drive I could sense she was terrified. She kept repeating as if a litany, what if something happens to my Daddy?

I could see her crying out of the corner of my eye. I told her to talk to Curtis about her fears. He'd be okay. I was sure of it. She talked to me about her Mom and I mentioned being adopted. So we formed a bond of sorts.

As I approached Curtis' house Retha's car was parked in the driveway. I gave Christine a big hug and assured her everything would be fine. I told her before she exited the car to feel free to call me. So the cold shoulder I received upon meeting her thawed. I was exhausted when I arrived home from multiple trips between the two suburbs. We lived nearly forty miles apart.

Curtis called later and thanked me for taking care of his baby. I told him it was no problem. I was sure he'd do the same for me if needed. A few months later, I went with Curtis to take Christine to the doctor's office. She had a yeast infection and was scared out of her wits.

Charles and I had always gotten along fairly well. Boys look at things differently from girls particularly Daddy's girls.

Di I felt it was only a matter of time before we'd eventually be together. Curtis shared his most prized possession with me. Entrusting his baby girl in my care. So I'm going to think this one through for myself. I can't ask anyone for his or her opinion. This is on me and I have to make the call for myself.

Do I think Curtis is playing me? Not really. But there's always that off chance. I guess I'm going to have to lay it on the line.

When the going gets rough I'll be there for you
Helping to support you in every little thing you do
In good times and bad yes I'm here
Cause that's what love is about my dear

May 30

When Curtis calls Di I'm going to ask again, about Retha's housing situation. When we finally connected he informed me she'd found an apartment. Retha was scheduled to go to the realtor's office tomorrow to begin the paperwork. I wanted to shout Hallelujah. Finally.

Curtis warned me not to get my hopes up because she'd done the same thing before.

My answer to that was, "my hopes are up and up they are going to stay. You have the eviction papers and know what to do to make this story have a happy ending."

He cautioned me again, "Just wait and see what happens."

Then he deftly changed the subject. "Do you remember my buddy Lenny? He was in an automobile accident and was hospitalized last night."

I said, "Sure I do. An accident? That's terrible."

I met Curtis and Lenny for breakfast a few months ago and I was nervous. After all he was after all Curtis' best friend. Lenny was charming and did his best to put me at ease. He worked for our company before I'd started working there. He was yet another old dog around Eddie's age. Lenny, Eddie and Curtis along with a couple of other guys go on a fishing trip once or twice a year.

The first year they fished while Curtis and I were dating was interesting. Curtis called me from his cell phone multiple times a day. We stayed in close contact. He said the guys were giving him the business about being whipped. He added it was all in good fun though. Lenny promised me after we met that if anything happened to Curtis he'd keep me in the loop.

Di if I'm honest with myself and I have to be at this point Retha is not leaving. She's not stupid and knows something is up. Sistah probably doesn't have one box or bag packed.

I should have pressed Curtis for details about their conversations. I know he's going to tell me tomorrow or on the first that she's not be leaving. I have to try and prepare myself for the worst. The time is almost upon us. I have to make a decision and do it quickly.

May 31

I'd actually planned to go to church this morning. But something always comes up whenever I try. My phone or pager goes off and it's always work. Most system changes are done in the wee hours on Sunday morning. So if I don't get a call by six o'clock, I just might be safe. Curtis called early this morning. He received a wake-up problem call from Operations. He asked yawning, "What do you have planned for the day?"

"I haven't decided yet, I might go to the city or stay home and watch basketball. "

The boys slept until one o'clock stumbling out of their bedrooms looking for something to eat.

Adele and Corrine called me on a three way. They'd finally getting around to quizzing me as to why Curtis didn't make it on Memorial Day. I had my pager in my hand. So I turned it off and on giving the impression it had gone off. I told them sorry. I've got to run duty calls.

The boys decided to spend the day with Gerry. So I had the house to myself. This should give me more time to reflect on my dilemma. I think I'm close to a solution.

Di in order for me to reach a logical conclusion, I had to document the good and bad. As you can tell it's been plenty of both. I find Debra an annoyance. I've always told Curtis if I felt like he and Retha were not going to go their separate ways then I'm out. I will not be in a triangle. No ifs, ands, or buts. It's not negotiable.

Sometimes I wonder if he's using Debra to make me jealous or force the issue? I don't know. I suspect he knows it's over and she's my replacement. The sneaking around with her bothers me. I know when he's lying to me. I can just sense it. I feel this entire month has been one lie after another.

I will get to the bottom of this. I will not go out like a punk. It will be hard working at the same place. I don't know if I can withstand the pressure. Maybe I consider

147

changing jobs. I know people will gossip especially if he ends up with Debra.

I remembered Eddie warning me about Curtis. Perhaps he knows something I don't. It's going to be ugly. Curtis called before I went to bed and reminded me that we wouldn't be meeting for lunch tomorrow. He had a team luncheon. We planned on meeting after work. Sweet dreams were the last words he said to me. Hah.

> The game of love can get rough you see
> So who's it gonna be *her she* or *me*
> The competition wears me out at times
> This man, his love, I can't seem to find

June 1

Di today's the first. I haven't heard a word from Curtis. It's still early though. What's a Sistah to do? I have tons of vacation/sick days accumulated. Maybe I'll call in sick. On second thought bump that. I'm going in. All was quiet on the work front. I had a team meeting myself but not a lunch one.

I met Curtis in the canteen for breakfast and then returned to my office. My meeting was scheduled at ten o'clock. Towards the close of the meeting the group does a round robin. We go around the table and give a status report on our projects. I was in a playful mood. Finally it was my turn.

Mark looked at me and asked, "Okay Marissa, what have you been working on this month?"

Visions of Curtis and myself in bed danced in my head. I answered innocently, "Nothing Mark. I've haven't done anything the entire month."

He looked at me with astonishment on his face. Then he and the team burst into laughter.

I quipped, "I've always wanted to say that and see your reaction."

When I finished my spiel Mark assigned me a couple of more projects.

The meeting was over at eleven. I decided to go to lunch early. Curtis' meeting started at eleven. So he had left already. I decided to make a detour to the ladies room first. On the way back to my office I bumped into one of his co-workers.

I asked, "Why are you still here? What happened to the meeting?"

Kevin replied, "It was cancelled." He went on to explain Sandy (their manager) had to leave due to a family emergency.

I walked back to my office and check voice mail. Nothing. I walked outside and noticed Curtis's car as well as Debra's gone. What the hell is this? I decided it was time for me to put on another cap. I switched out of data processing mode and into Ms. Detective.

I drove to Arby's and bought a chicken sandwich. Then parked strategically near the building. I'd be able to see cars coming and going. An hour late I hit pay dirt. Curtis drove towards the building and five minutes later Debra followed. I couldn't believe what my eyes had just shown me.

I drove back to work in a daze not really seeing anything around me. I don't know how I made it back to the office. I checked voice mail and there was a message from Curtis. He explained his meeting had been cancelled. He knew I was attending my staff meeting. So he was heading out to lunch and would call me later. I called him sweetness and light in my voice.

Curtis didn't have a clue as to the storm that would erupt later. At two thirty I called him again and asked if he'd meet me at the forest preserve. I gave an academy winning performance. Lord knows I've had years of practice.

There was no shame in my game. In reality Di I felt as if my world was crumbling, like brittle, stale toast. But I knew I had to remain strong. More important it was finally time to let go.

The words Eddie had said to me two weeks ago came back to haunt me. I knew he was telling the truth. It may have seemed like I was in denial. In reality I wasn't.

I left the building blindly since my eyes didn't want to cooperate and remain dry. I sat in my car and composed myself. I had to get it together for the big showdown.

Ten minutes later I returned to my desk with my professional face intact. Finally I left work at two fifty. As I drove to the forest preserves the tears began to flow. Memories flooded my mind like the gates of a dam being opened. We'd shared so many good and bad times. For instance Curtis drove me to the hospital from work when Gerry Jr. was hit by automobile. Thank God he'd didn't suffer any life-threatening injuries just a few broken bones. And bumps and bruises. That was one of the scariest moments of my life.

I remember celebrating Curtis and my first sweetest day. He called and asked me to meet him in the canteen. It seemed he took forever to meet me there. I'd just about given up hope of him putting in an appearance and stood to head back to my office. Very irritated I might add. I took a few steps away from the table when the telephone in the canteen rang.

Curtis asked if I'd run back to my desk and bring today's paper back with me. Di I must have called him everything except a child of God. I flounced back to my desk and the scent of a floral bouquet hit me before I stepped into my office.

Babyface's song, '*Every time I Close My Eyes*', summed up my feeling for Curtis. I'd purchased the cd

151

during lunch. When I returned to work and listened to the song it brought tears to my eyes. I called Curtis and asked him to come to my office ASAP. I put the headphones in his ears and asked him to listen. He asked if I was crying. I told him it was the most beautiful song I'd ever heard. He proclaimed it our song.

Di the day my divorce was granted Curtis and I had plans. We were finally going to consummate the relationship. I hadn't had sex in four years and I was good, hot, wet, and ready. You've heard of Murphy's Law or the best-laid plans right? That saying became applicable and more. I'd bought myself a sexy little black dress and matching shoes. Let's not forget the Victoria Secrets lingerie. I'd made reservations at the Embassy Suites hotel.

After leaving court I stopped home and picked up my overnight bag. Then drove to the hotel and checked in. I was so happy because today promised to be one of the best days of my life. Imagine my shame and anger when Mother Nature put in an appearance. I couldn't believe it when my period started then stopped.

Curtis called a couple of times during the day and I didn't have to the heart to tell him our plans may come to naught. He arrived after work. I greeted him at the door. He held a yellow rose in one hand and a bottle of champagne in the other. He remarked lightly that he wasn't sure if flowers were appropriate or not.

We kissed for eons it seemed. His hands began roaming and sure enough he felt the dreaded pad. I burst into tears. He told me not to worry that he was sure the hotel had plenty of towels. Luckily we didn't need them. I was touched that he cared enough to even go there.

As they say Di he rocked my world. We knocked boots and it was quite good. We ordered room service and he fed me. I swear Di my heart swelled full of love. No man had ever showered so much attention on me. It's the memories that get you every time. How am I going to let all of that go?

Finally it was time. Curtis pulled his car next to mine and got out of his car with a somber look on his face. He could see the truth on mine. The usual greetings your place or mine weren't uttered. I sighed got out of my car and asked him if we could walk.

We strolled along a little path and stood silently.

Then I asked about Retha. "Has she actually signed papers for an apartment yet?"

He replied, "No, she hasn't. Not yet. There's a problem with her credit. Don't worry she's still moving."

I sighed, "Has she packed anything? Any of her possessions."

"No but it's not like she has that much to pack anyway."

"Let me guess you're still sleeping in the bed with her too?"

He said, "Yes but there's nothing going on anyway. You know I sleep in the basement most of the time Rissa."

I nodded my head sadly. Di I couldn't leave Debra out. "One more question then I'm done. What happened at lunchtime? How come you didn't wait for me?"

"Well," he said dropping his head. "I had lunch with Debra. I had the phone in my hand to call you. She walked into my office and pressured me into having lunch with her.

"She pressured you? I echoed as my mouth fell open. "It seems you have a hard time telling women NO. Other than me that is."

He held his hands out, "Baby it didn't mean anything."

"If it didn't mean anything Curtis," I said toe-to-toe with him. "Then you would have called me and left a message before you left with her. Let's see where we are here." I added as I pointed my finger in his face. "You can't just say no to Debra and can't get Retha out of your house. " My foot tapped impatiently and my arms were folded across my chest. "You aren't leaving me with anything to work with here. You seem incapable of just saying NO." I screamed.

He replied, "You're overreacting. Now just calm down."

I yelled, "Oh but you're wrong. I'm definitely calm and I know what I have to do. How would you feel," I cried. My face was red and tear stained. "If you were in my place? How would you feel Curtis knowing I live with someone else and slept next to him every single night? Would it make you feel good if I went to lunch with another man and didn't leave you a message? HOW WOULD IT FEEL?" My voice seemed to get louder and higher.

His face seemed to sag with each word from my mouth. He attempted to grab me. But I wasn't having it and pulled away from him.

"I'll tell you how you'd feel Curtis. Bad. You'd feel like your feelings don't count and you're nothing. You know what else Curtis, I don't ever intend to feel this way again over someone else's man. Because that's who you are Curtis Retha's man maybe even Debra's too. I promise you that I won't ever forget it again."

He pulled me into his arms sorrowfully. I cried earnestly.

"Shhh," he murmured, his voice breaking, "I'm sorry Baby I didn't mean to hurt you. That was never my intention. Rissa you know I love you."

I put my hand across his mouth quieting him. "Curtis, you and I both know it's over." I said as tears streamed from my eyes.

He looked dejected and shook his head as if to say how did we get to this point. He continued to hold me until I calmed down. We kissed for what seemed an eternity and he held me in his arms a long time. Finally I pushed away looked into his eyes and said simply, "It's over."

Curtis stared at me for a time. Grief contorted his face. He tried to pull me back into his arms. Curtis growled, "I don't think so Rissa. Not by a long shot. We'll get through this."

I shook my head, "Just leave. Go Curtis. I want to be alone."

He hugged me one more time. Then got into his car and drove screeching out the parking lot. I got into my car and laid my head against the steering wheel and cried my heart out. The tears seemed endless. I knew hard times lie ahead of me. After all we worked in the same building. Not to mention I'd have to contend with Debra's smirking face.

The curtain had been lifted from my eyes. Our relationship was really over. Later I started my car and put it into gear. Then pulled out of the parking lot. Tomorrow yes it's another day. I'll just have to remain strong and keep the faith. I won't give in no matter what Curtis says or does. There are other fish in the sea. I'm like a Timex watch I can take a licking and keep on ticking. It's finally time for me to move on.

When it's over, I said I would know
When I'd had enough and it was time to go
I wouldn't hang on and prolong the agony
I would just walk away, head held high, you see

Di peace out. It's a wrap.

HALLELUJAH!!!!!

Marissa Walters

Discussion Guide

1. Do you think Marissa was naïve in her expectations of the relationship between her and Curtis? Was she reading the signs correctly that Curtis sent her on the state of the relationship?

2. Should ultimatums be given in relationships when there are issues?

3. Was Curtis playing Marissa or do you think he had genuine love or feelings for her?

4. Were Curtis and Marissa correct in exposing their children to their relationship?

5. Do you feel Curtis really gave Retha an ultimatum to leave or was he just saying that to string Marissa along?

6. Do you think Retha was aware that Curtis was cheating on her?

7. Do you think women in general can sense when their man is cheating?

8. Was Marissa's family influential in her choice of men and the decisions she made in life?

9. Should Marissa have confronted her family about her feelings and issues with them? Do you think she was overly sensitive about her sisters?

10. Do you think Marissa was in denial about her family issues and in turn this caused her to be lenient about her relationship with Curtis?

11. What are some of the reasons women get involved with married men or men in committed relationships?
12. Do you think Curtis was involved with Debra?
13. Should Marissa have given Curtis more time to remove Retha from his house if his intentions were honest?
14. Marissa wrote poetry to express her feelings for Curtis. Do you feel that technique aided in explaining her story more effectively?
15. Was the use of the poetry combined with the diary, helpful in understanding Marissa emotions?

Michelle Larks really appreciates your support and would love to hear from you. You can send her comments, ask questions, request autographed copies and invite her to read at your next event
Send an e-mail to

MichelleLarks@COMCAST.NET

and visit

www.MichelleLarks.com

Ordering Information

Myriad of Emotions by Michelle Larks

In Stores: ISBN: 0-9722795-2-0
On-Line at www.Amazon.com
On-Line at www.EbonyEnergyPublishing.com
On-Line at www.MichelleLarks.com

Crisis Mode by Michelle Larks

Crisis Mode **is a collection of short stories about four women facing dilemmas as they come to crossroads in their lives. All are faced with tough decisions and choices as they manage to cope and overcome diversities. For sample chapters please visit**

www.MichelleLarks.com

Michelle Larks

Was born and raised in the Windy City and currently resides in a suburb near Chicago along with her husband. She is the proud mother of two lovely daughters attending college.

Michelle had published a poem in the book, *Seasons Change,* **as part of a series sponsored by the International Library of Poetry. She has written poetry for her company's newsletter's celebrating Black History month.**

Michelle has been employed in the data processing field for over twenty years and is currently working on her next project Mirrored Images.